HYMNS 4 WORSHIP
AMAZING GRACE

Transcriptions and Engravings by Brent Roberts

All Creatures Of Our God And King

Performed by Slater Armstrong

St. FRANCIS OF ASSISI
Translated by William H. Draper

Geistliche Kirchengasänge, Cologne, 1623
Harmonized by Ralph Vaughn Williams

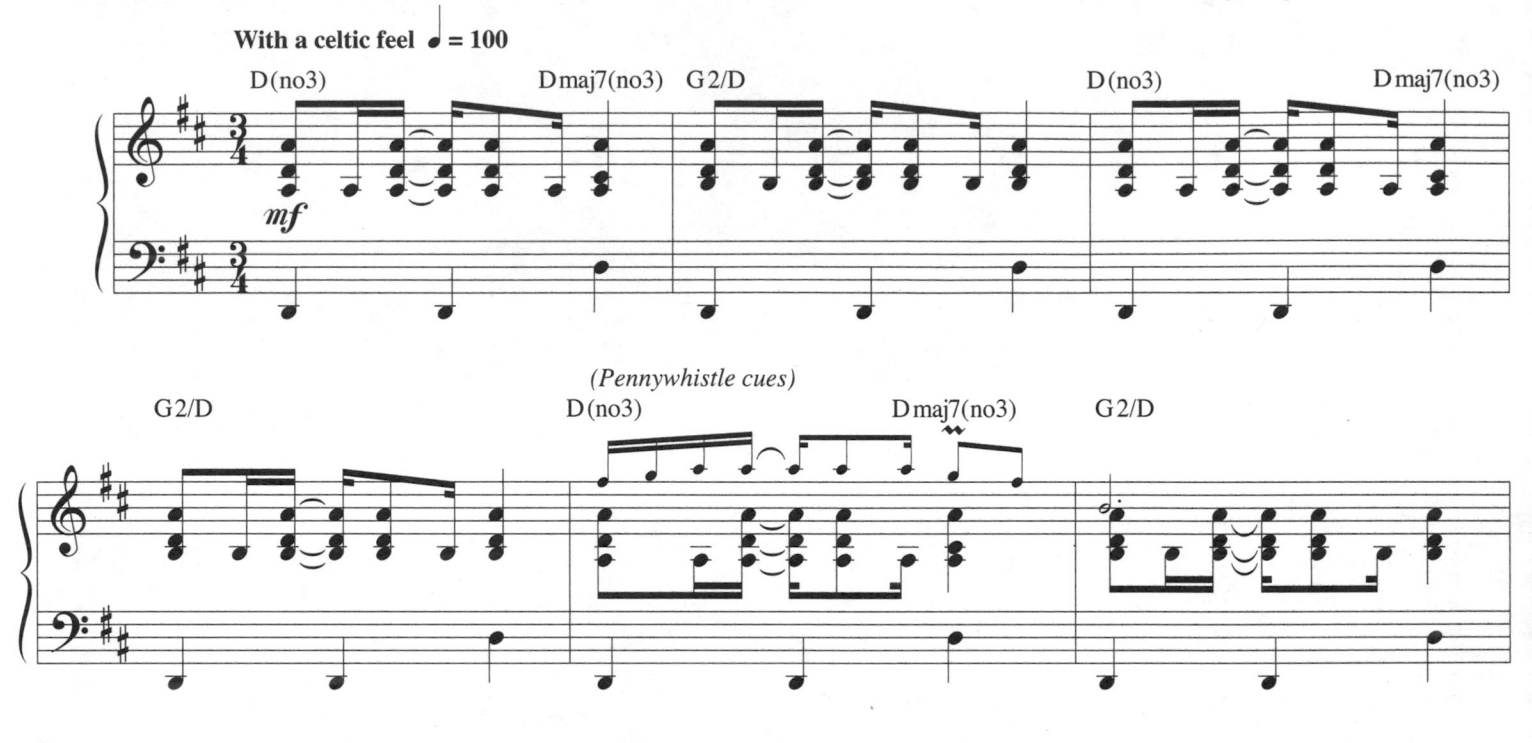

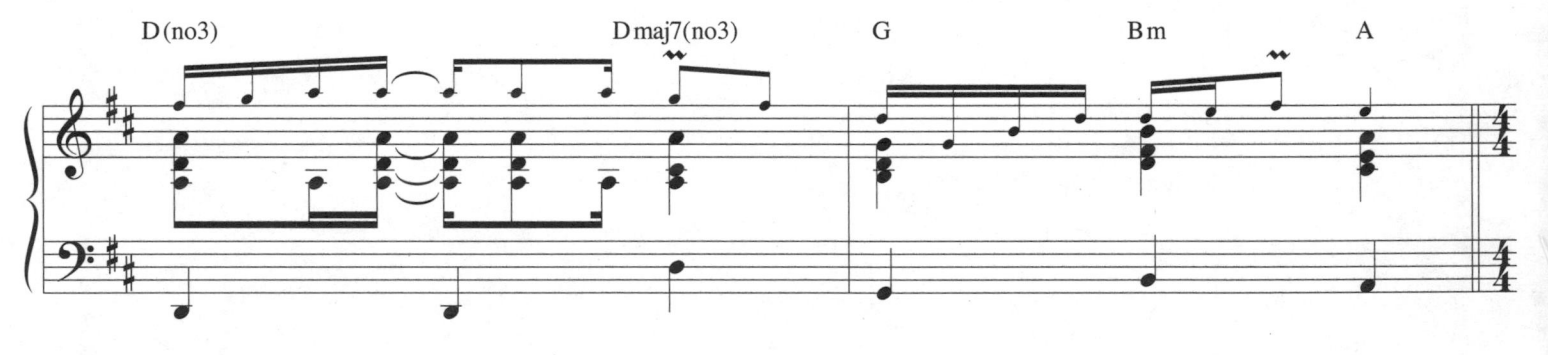

1. All crea - tures of our God and King,
2. Thou rush - ing wind that art so strong,

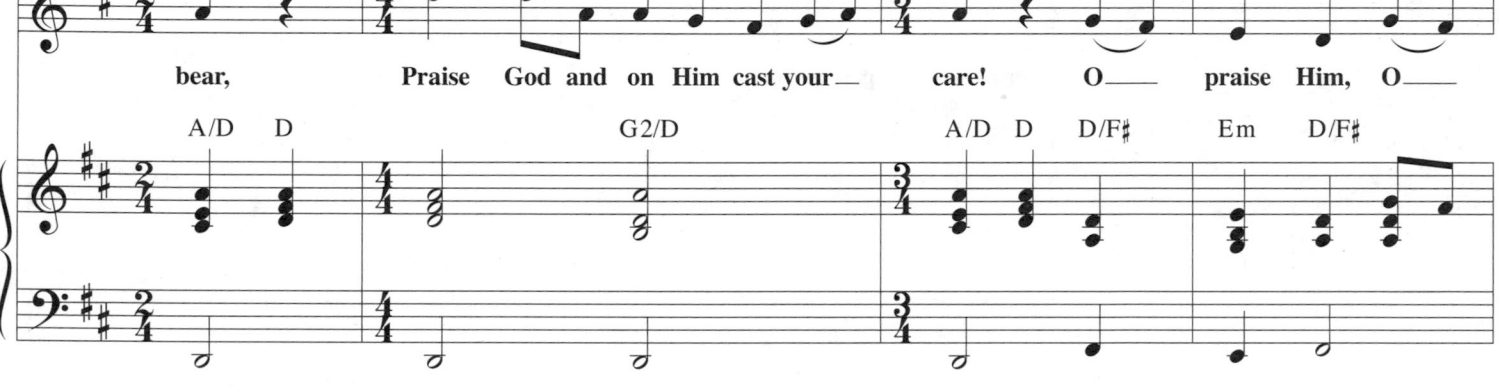

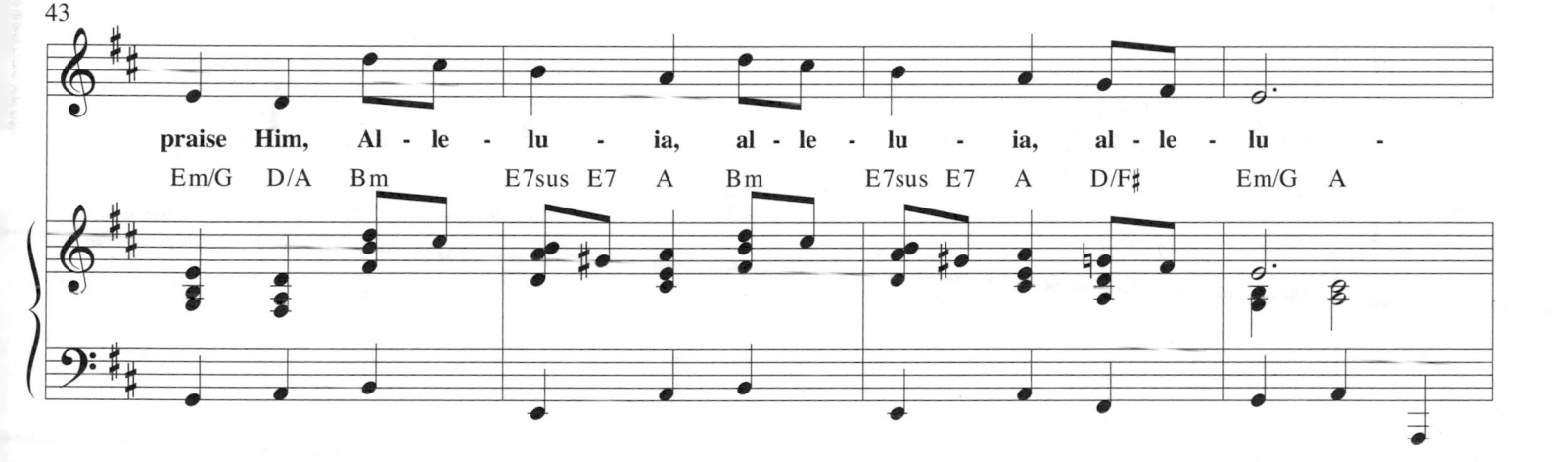

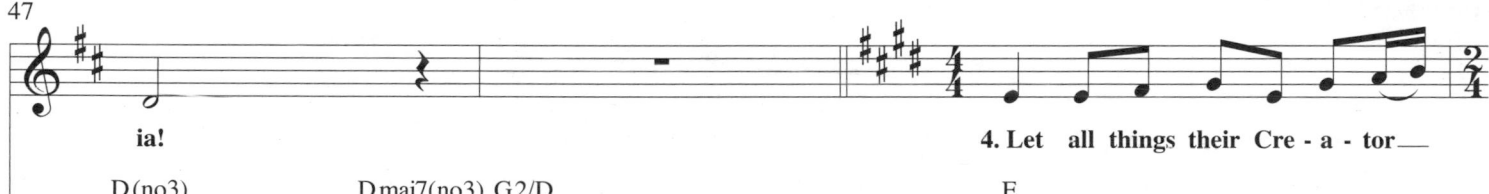

64
ia!
E2(no3)
67
E(no3)
Emaj7(no3)
A2/E
70
Al - le, al - le - lu -
E(no3)
Emaj7(no3)
A
C♯m
B
E(no3)
Emaj7(no3)
73
All crea - tures of our God and King,
ia.
A2/E
E(no3)
Emaj7(no3)
A2/E

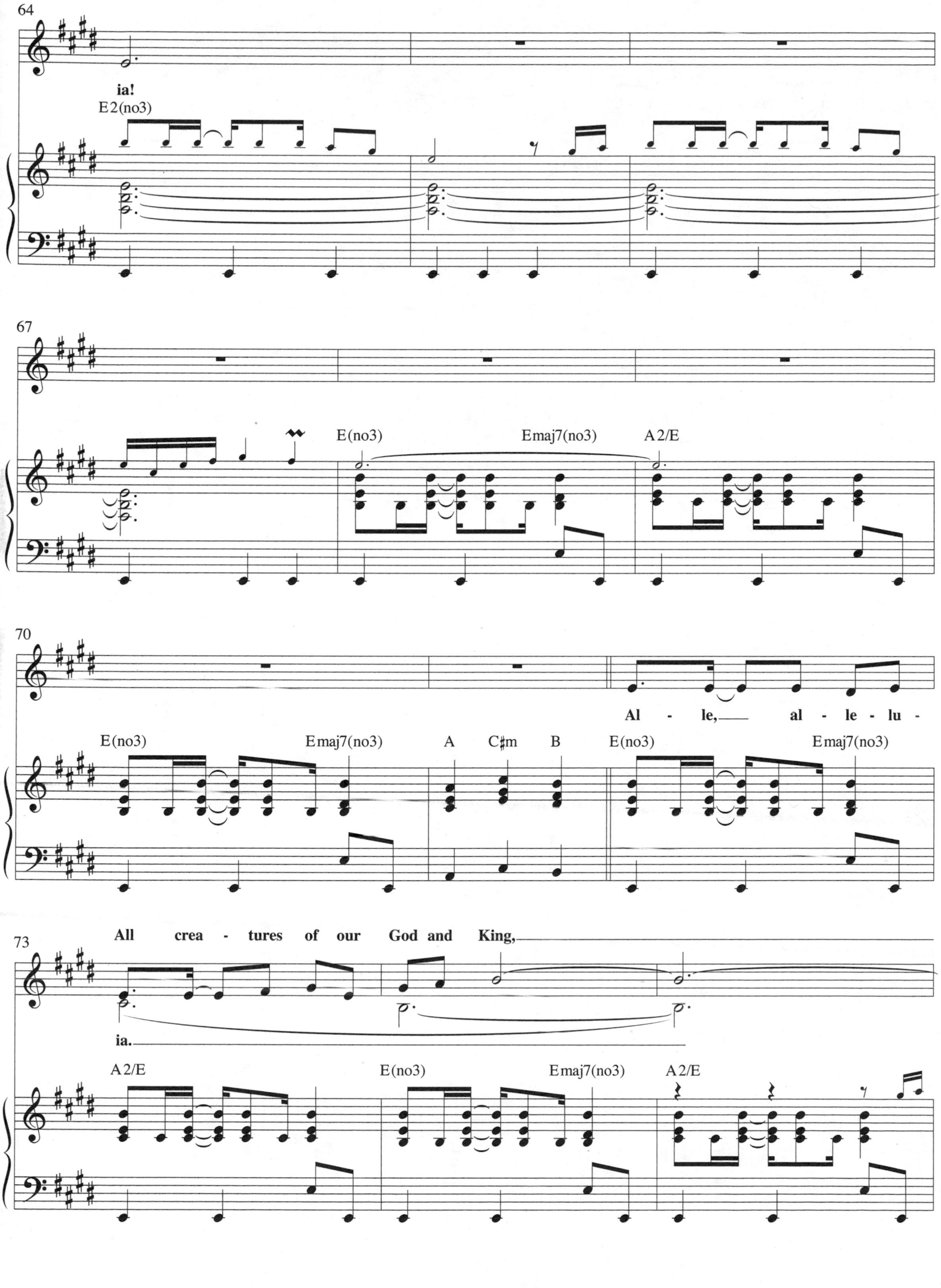

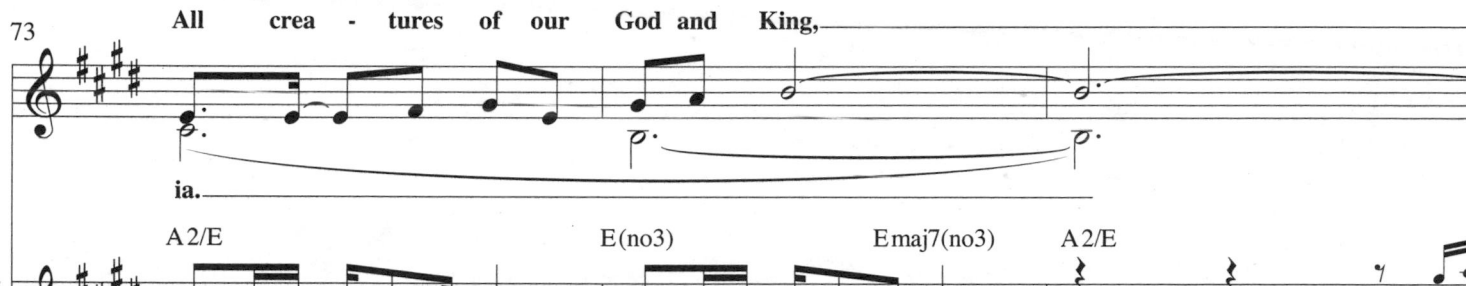

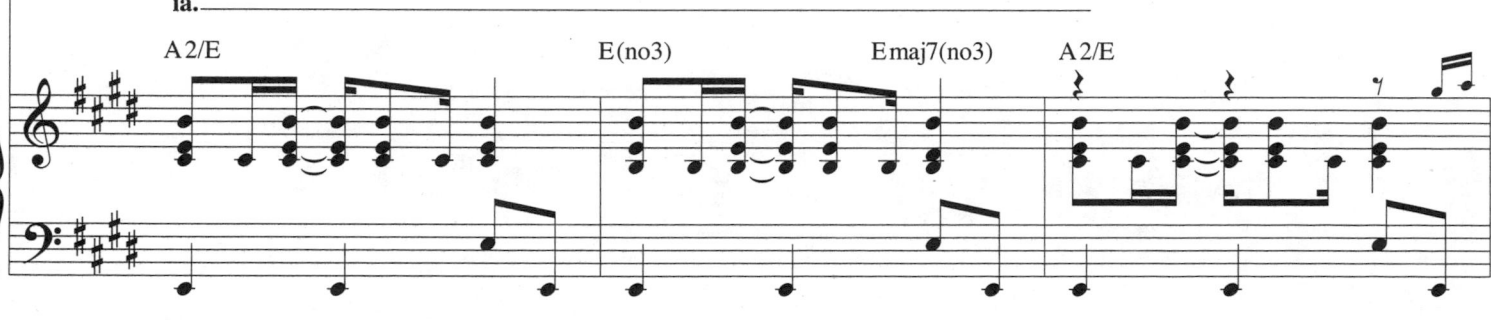

No, Not One

Performed by Lenny LeBlanc

JOHNSON OATMAN, JR.   **GEORGE C. HUGG**

With conviction! ♩ = 100

(Drum lead-in)

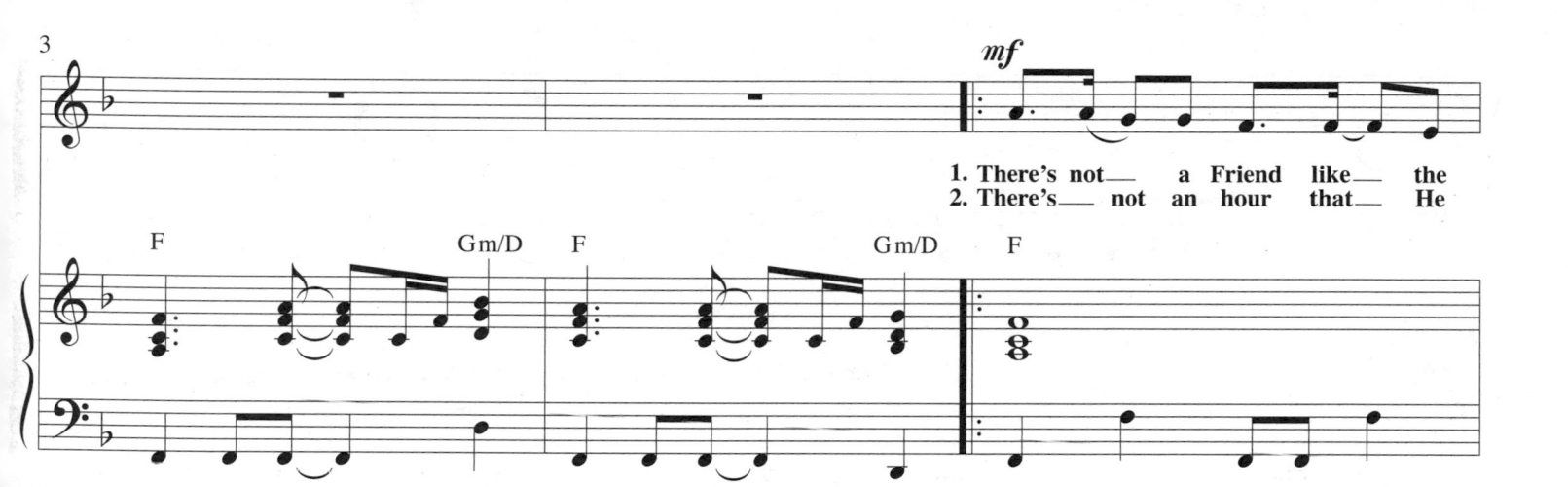

1. There's not___ a Friend like___ the
2. There's___ not an hour that___ He

low - ly Je - sus.   No, not___ one!   No,___ not___ one!
is not near___ us,   No, not___ one!   No,___ not___ one!

Come, Thou Fount Of Every Blessing

Performed by Sara Groves

ROBERT ROBINSON;
Adapted by Margaret Clarkson

TRADITIONAL AMERICAN MELODY
JOHN WYETH'S *Repository of Sacred Music, 1813*

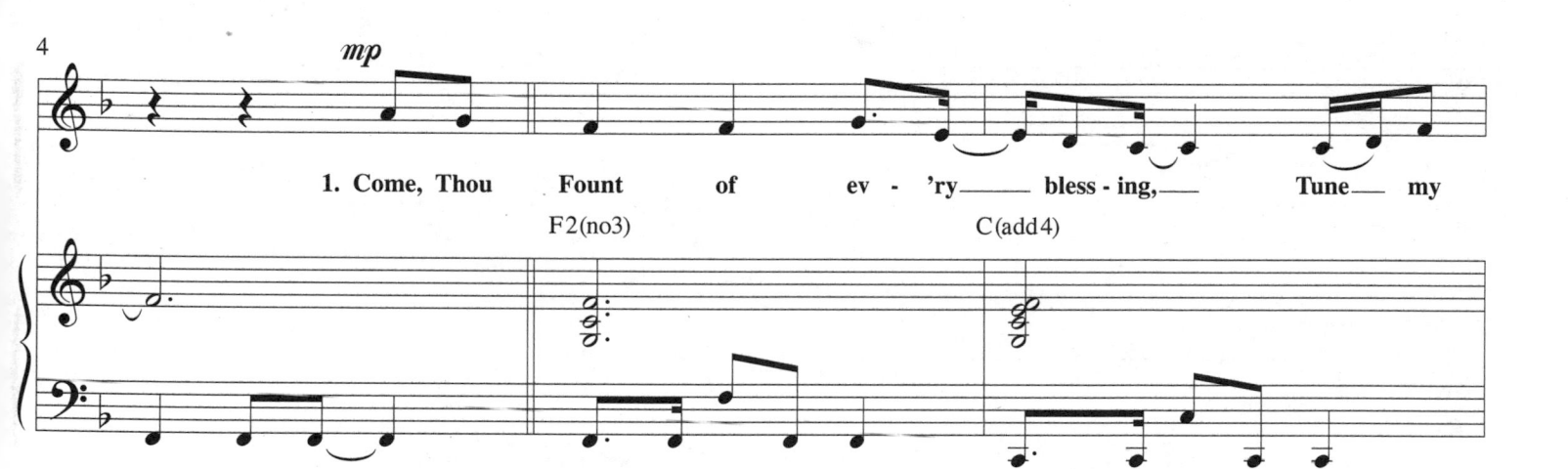

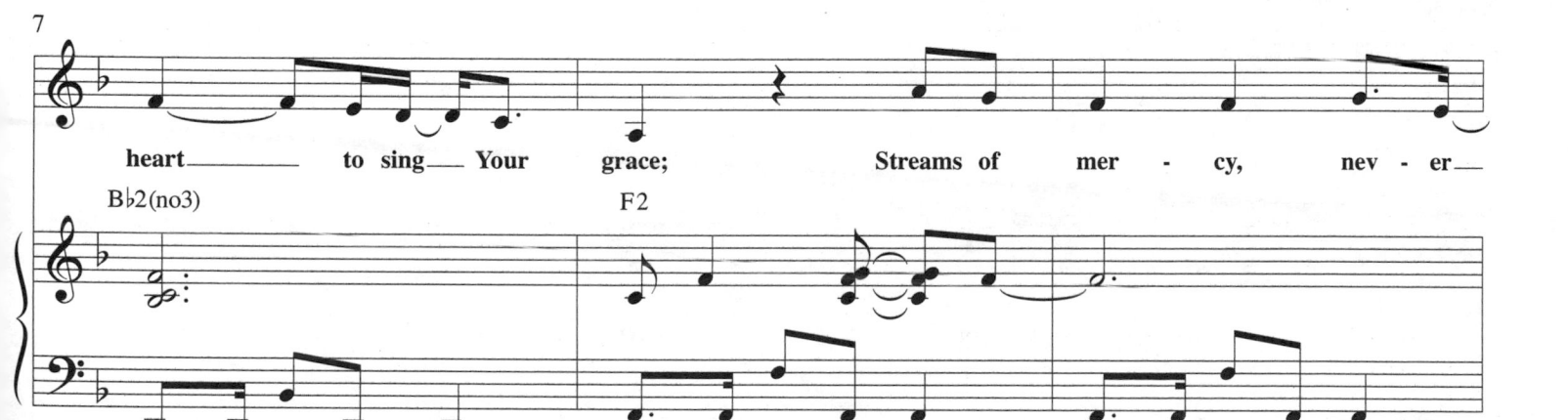

The Solid Rock

Performed by 4Him

EDWARD MOTE

WILLIAM B. BRADBURY

Pop rock ♩ = 116

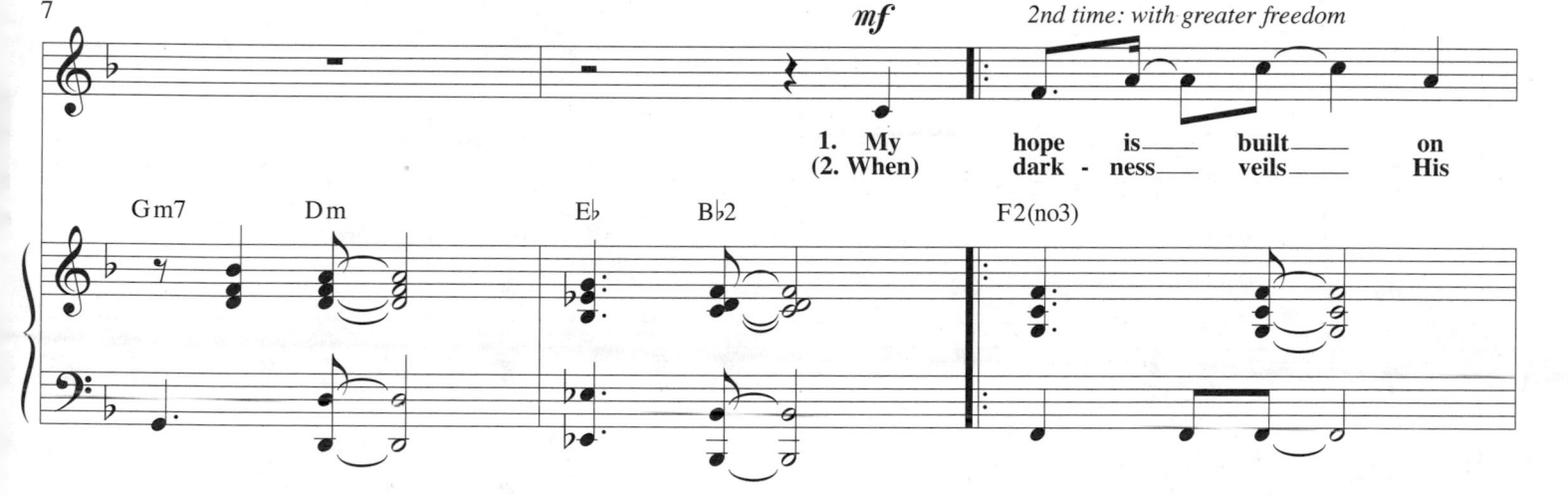

2nd time: with greater freedom

1. My hope is built on nothing less Than Jesus' blood and righteousness. I
(2. When) darkness veils His lovely face, I rest on His unchanging grace. Through

37

The sol - id Rock.—

Dm7   B♭2(no3)

40

The sol - id Rock.—

F/A   B♭2(no3)   Dm

43

Ooo,———   ah.

f

B♭maj7   G/B   C

f

46

The sol - id Rock.—

Em   C

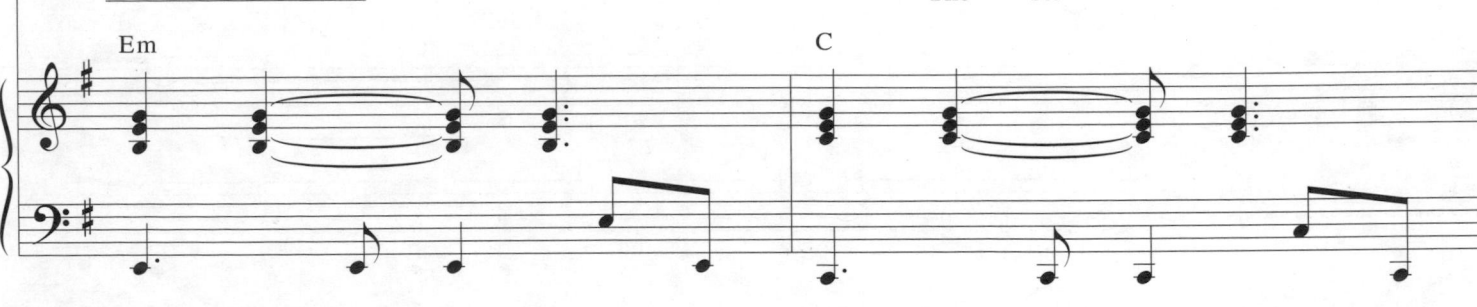

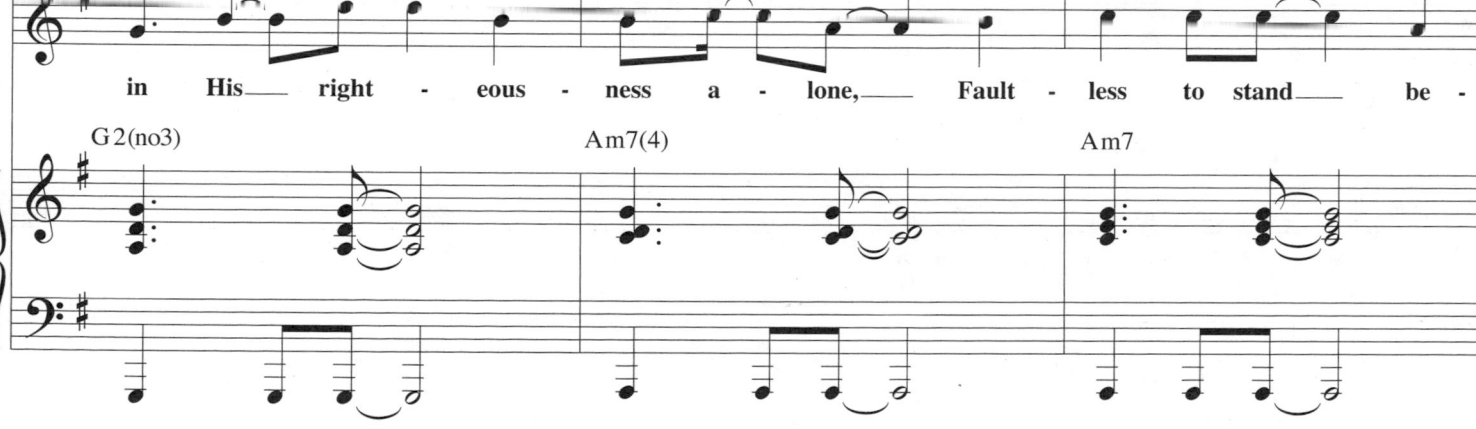

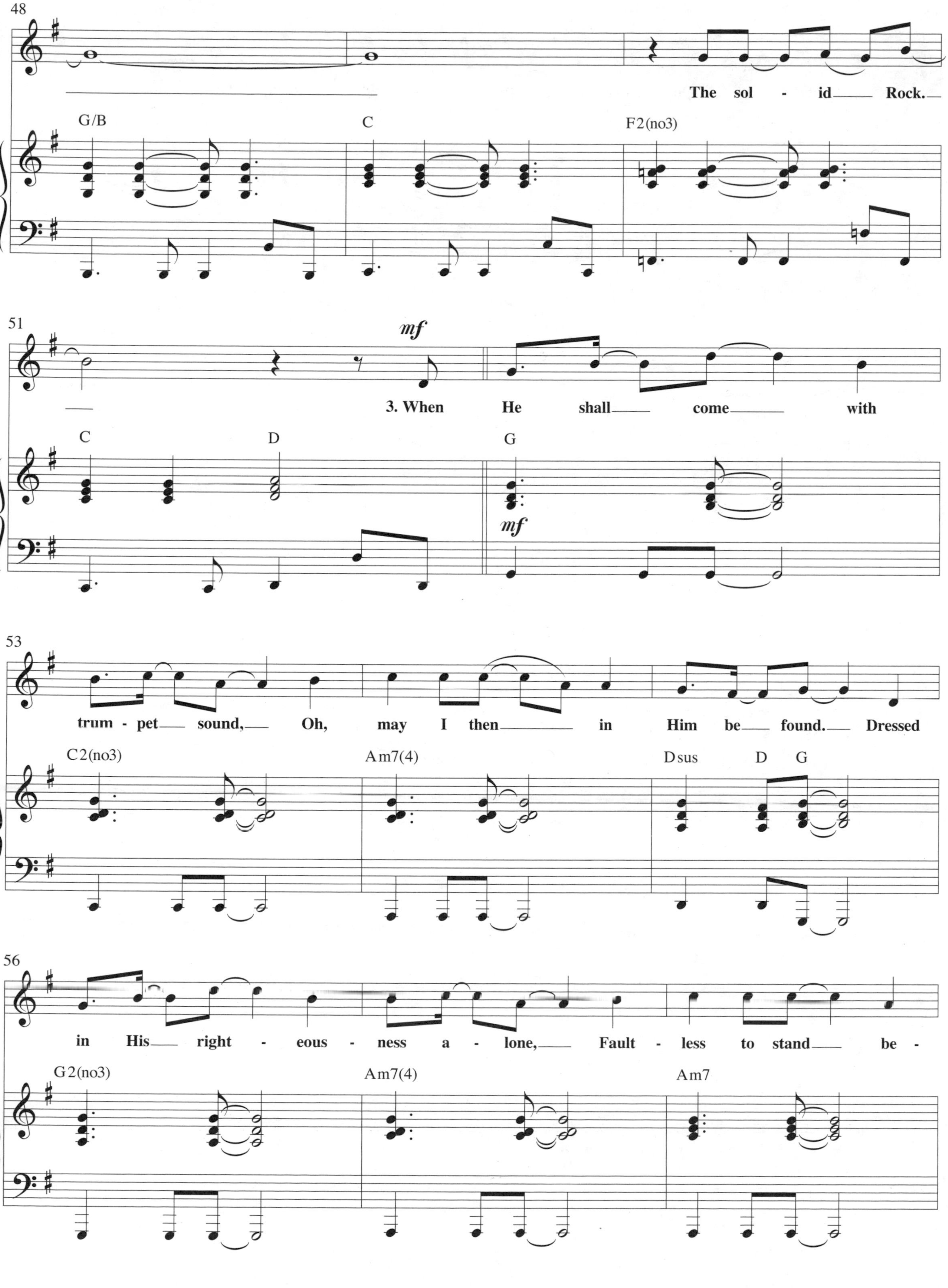
48
G/B
C
F2(no3)
The sol - id Rock.
51
mf
3. When He shall come with
C
D
G
mf
53
trum - pet sound, Oh, may I then in Him be found. Dressed
C2(no3)
Am7(4)
Dsus
D
G
56
in His right - eous - ness a - lone, Fault - less to stand be -
G2(no3)
Am7(4)
Am7

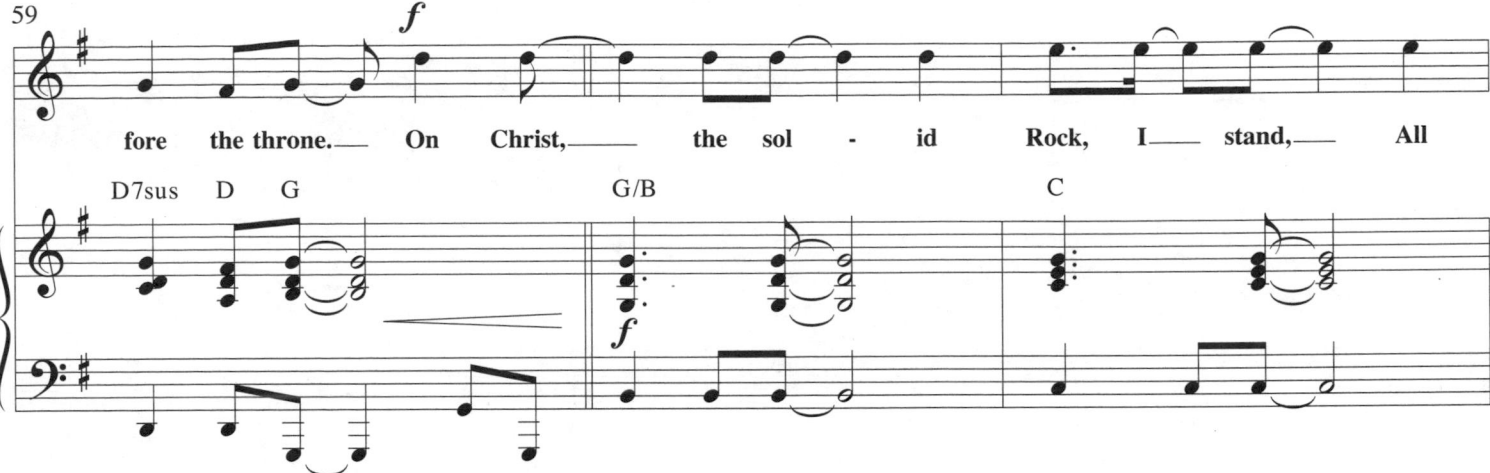

59

fore the throne.— On Christ,— the sol - id Rock, I— stand,— All

D7sus D G   G/B   C

62

oth - er— ground— is sink - ing sand; All—

G/B   Em   A9   Dsus   D

(cues optional)

65

oth - er— ground,— all— oth - er— ground,— all— oth - er - ground— is

C2(no3) G2/B   C2(no3) G2/B   C2(no3) G2/B

68

sink - ing— sand.— The sol - id Rock, on

F2(no3) Am7/D   G/B   F C

Fairest Lord Jesus

Performed by Amy Grant

ANONYMOUS GERMAN HYMN, *Münster Gesangbuch, 1677*

TRADITIONAL
Schlesische Volkslieder, 1842

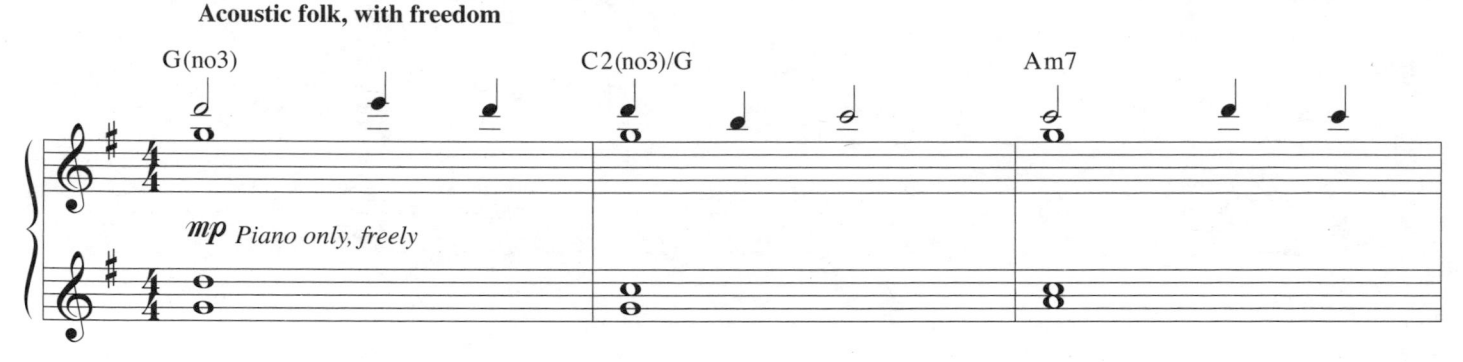

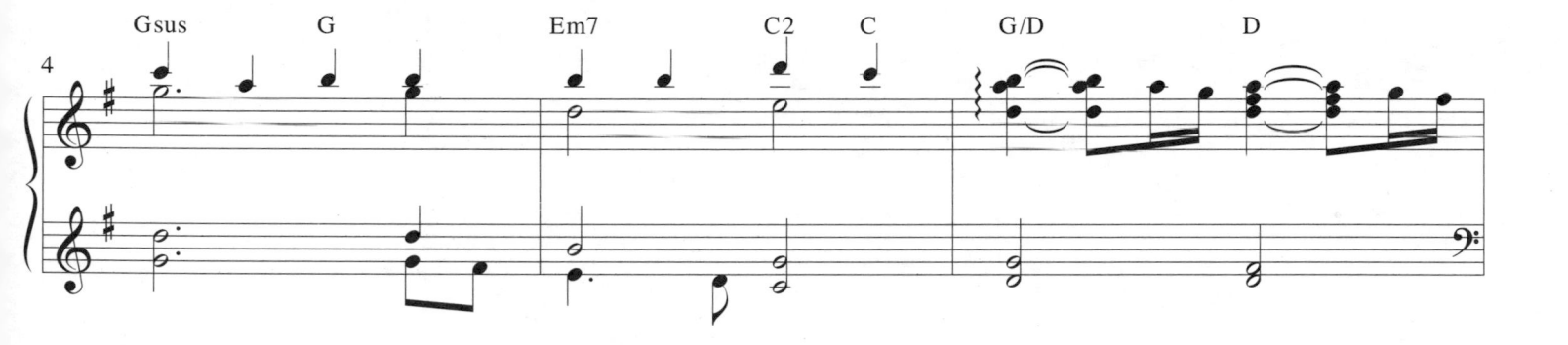

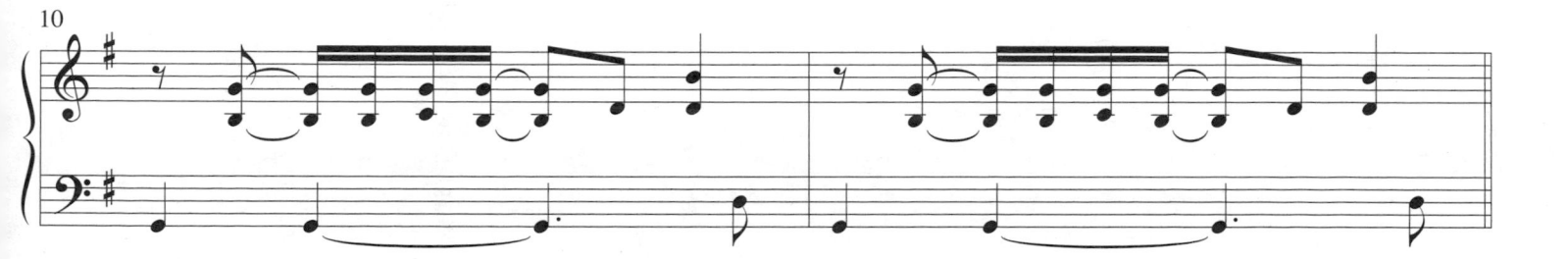

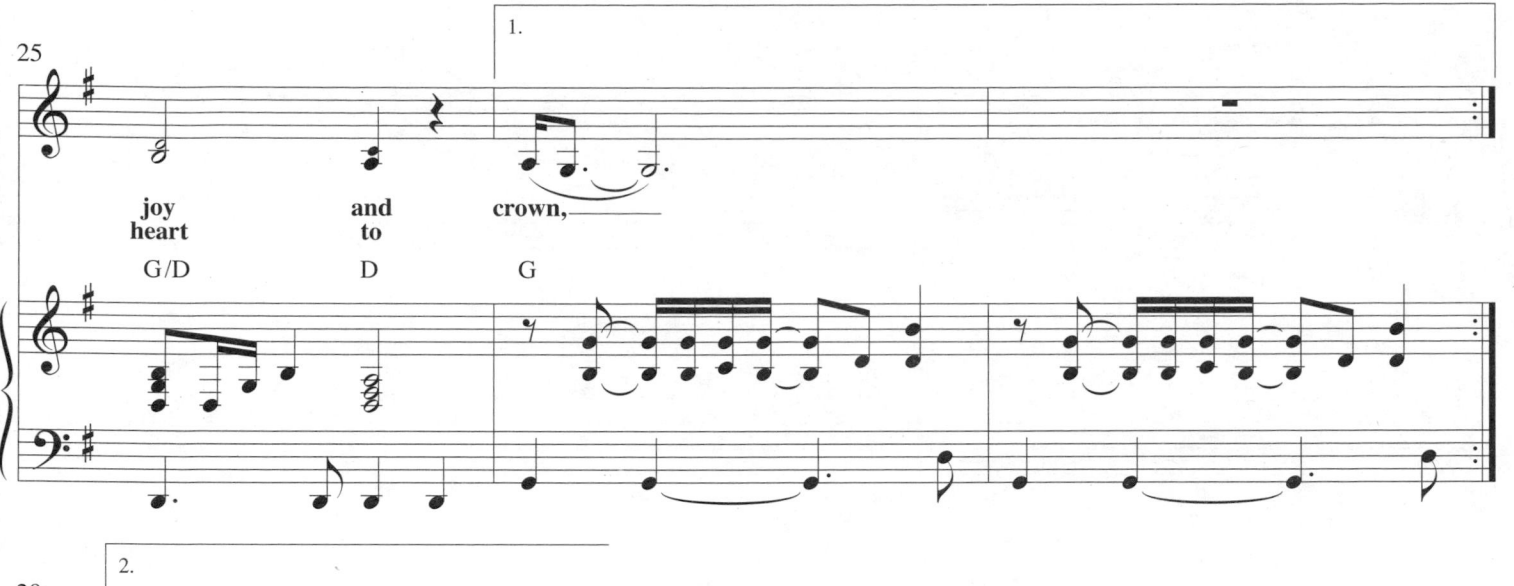

joy and crown,_____
heart to

G/D   D   G

sing._____

G   C   G

C   G   C   G

C   G   C   G

G7

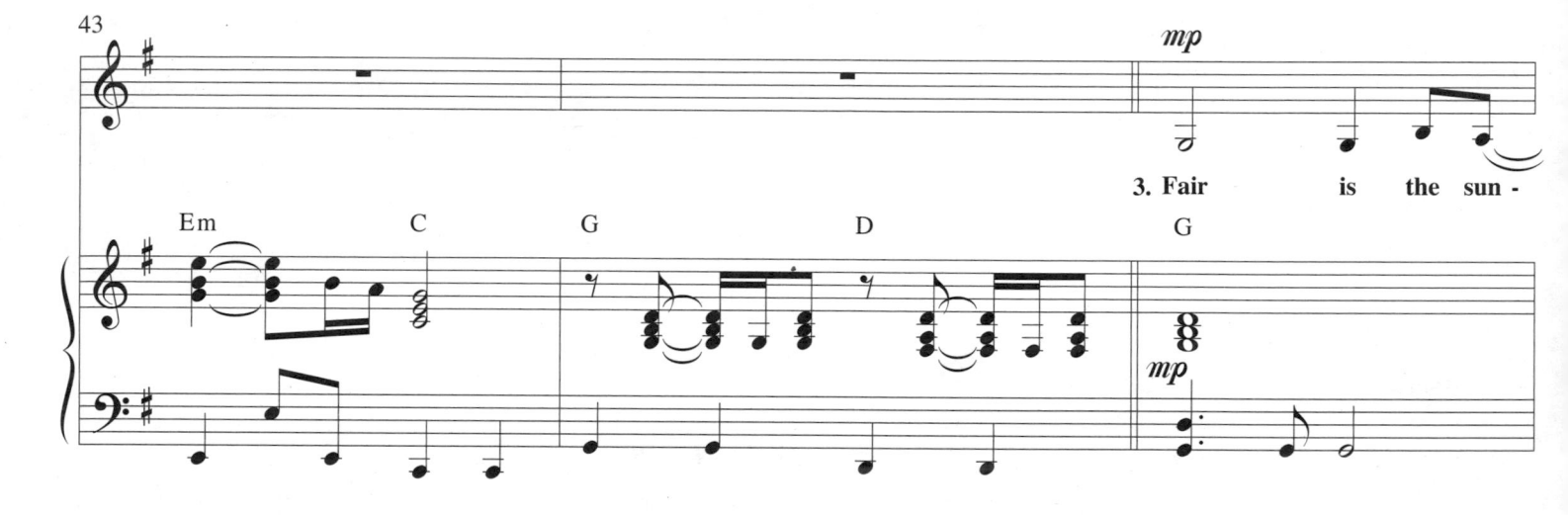

3. Fair is the sun -

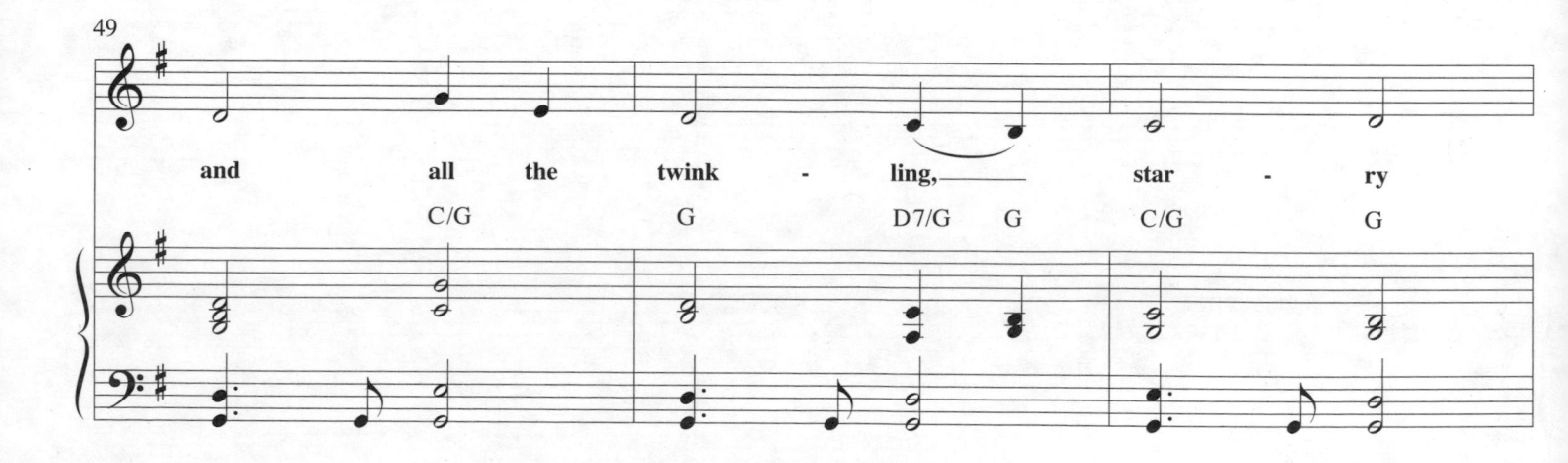

- shine; ___ Fair - er still ___ the moon - light ___

and all the twink - ling, ___ star - ry

A Mighty Fortress Is Our God

Performed by Brian Doerksen

Words and Music by
MARTIN LUTHER

With strength ♩ = 96

1. A might-y for-tress is___ our___
(2. If) we in our___ own strength con-

God, A strong-hold nev-er fail-
fide, Our striv-ing will be los-

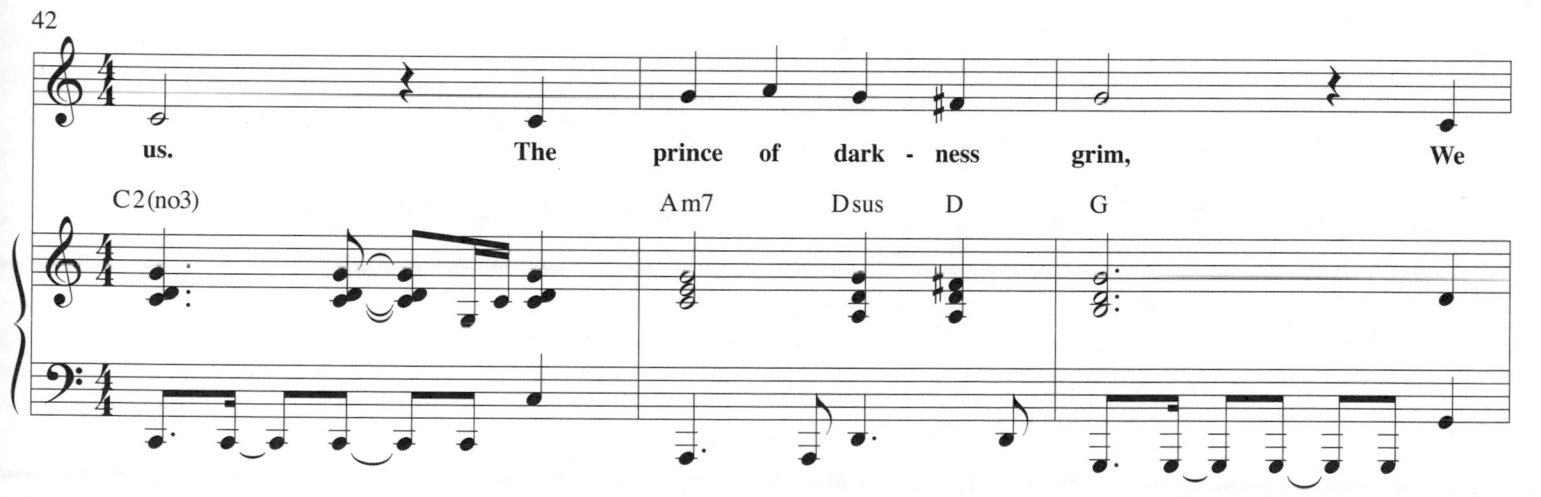

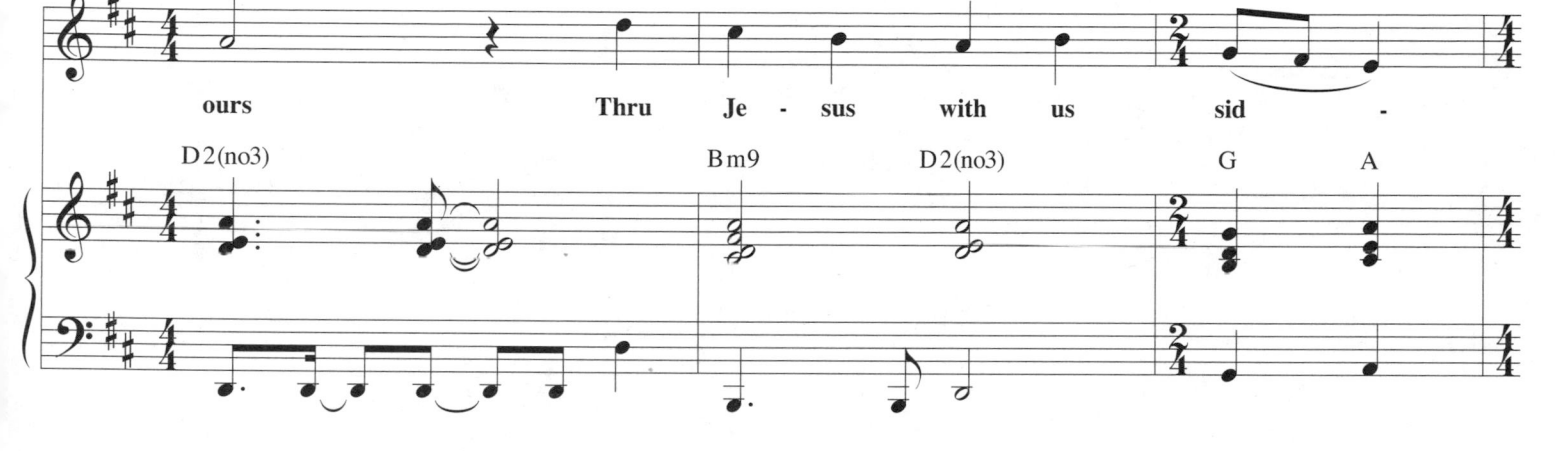

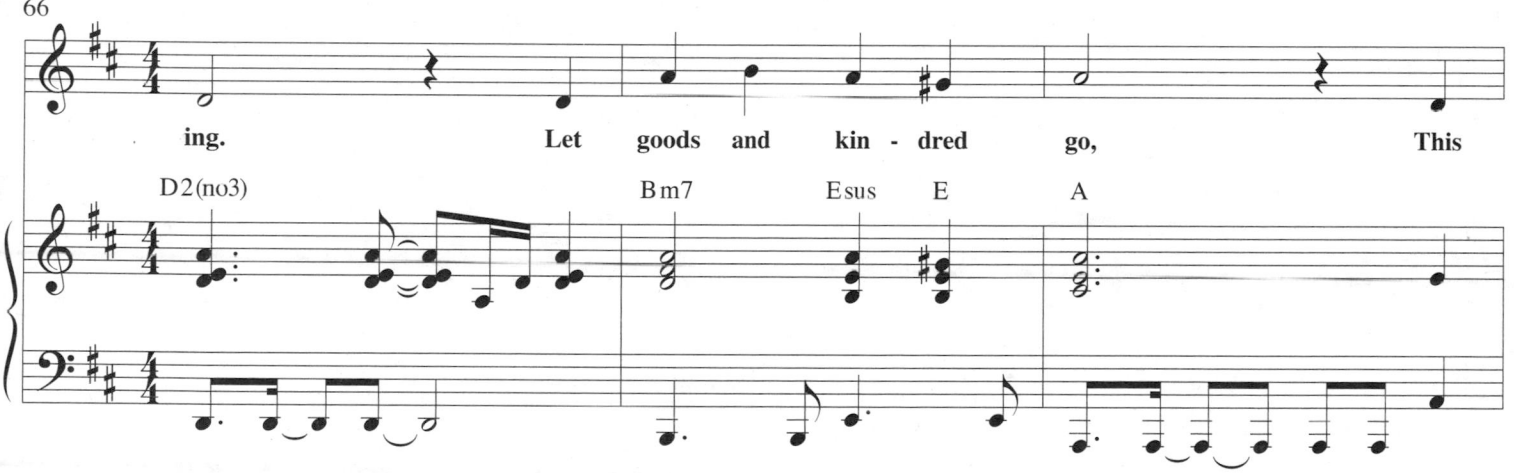

The Love Of God

Performed by Mercy Me

Words and Music by
FREDERICK M. LEHMAN
Arranged by Jim Bryson, Nathan Cochran,
Peter Kipley, Bart Millard, Robby Shaffer
and Mike Scheuchzer

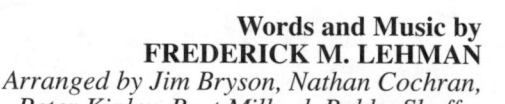

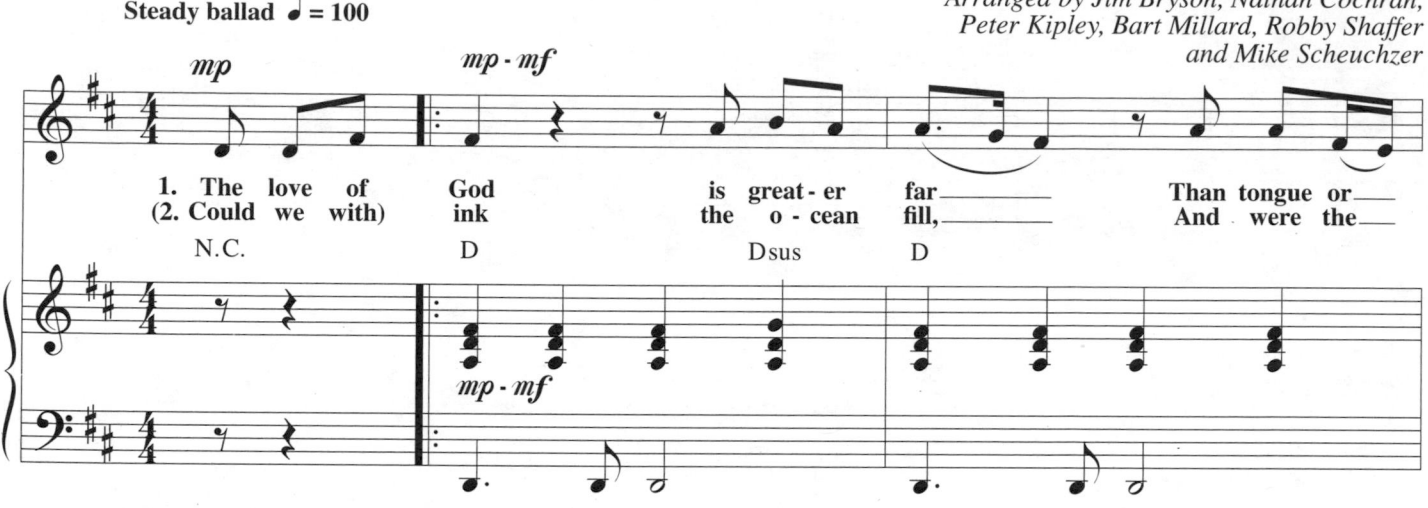

Holy, Holy, Holy! Lord God Almighty

Performed by Paul Baloche

REGINALD HEBER

JOHN B. DYKES

Turn Your Eyes Upon Jesus

Performed by Michael W. Smith

**Words and Music by
HELEN H. LEMMEL**
Arranged by Michael W. Smith

Worshipfully, with great freedom ♩ = 80

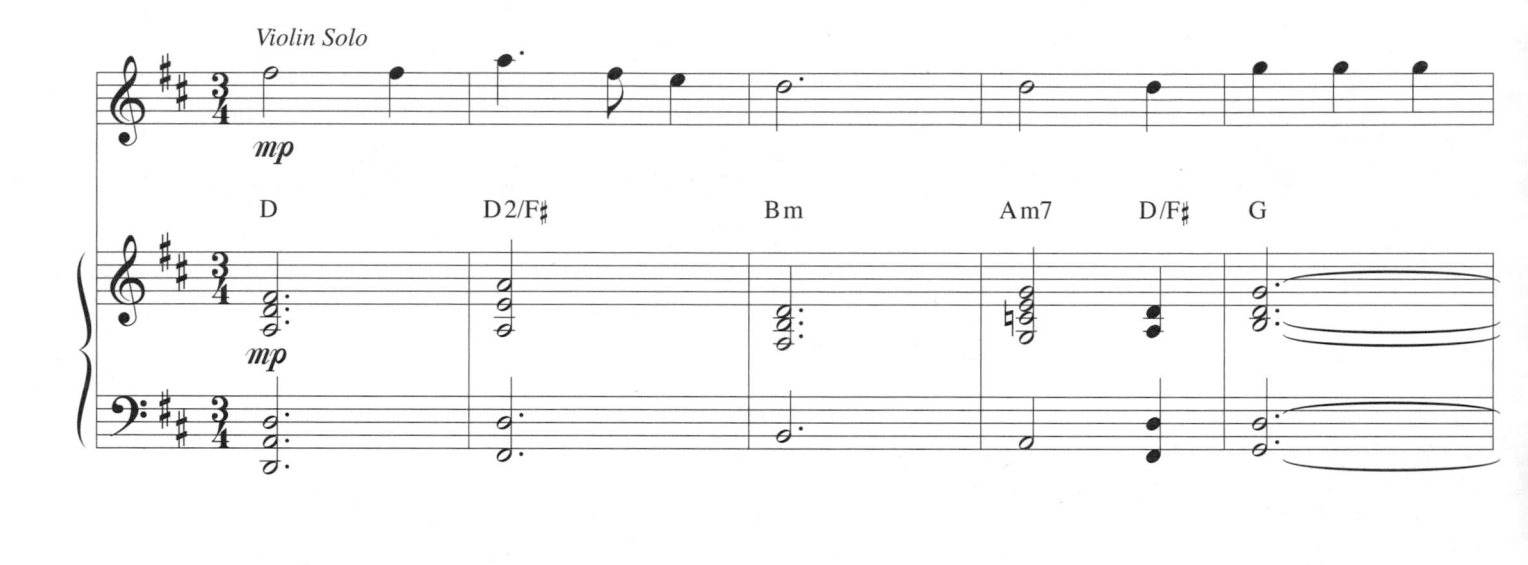

How Great Thou Art

Performed by Eoghan Heaslip

Words and Music by
STUART K. HINE

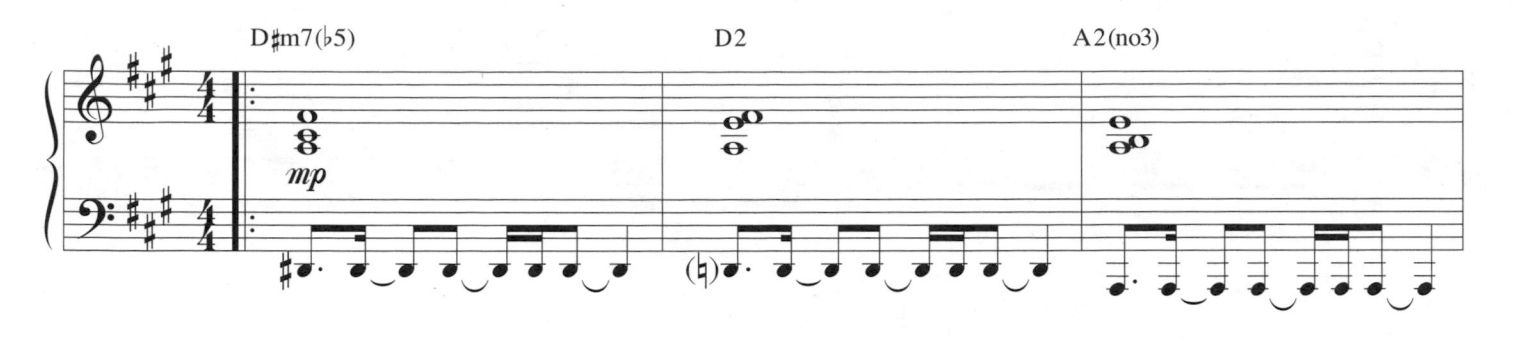

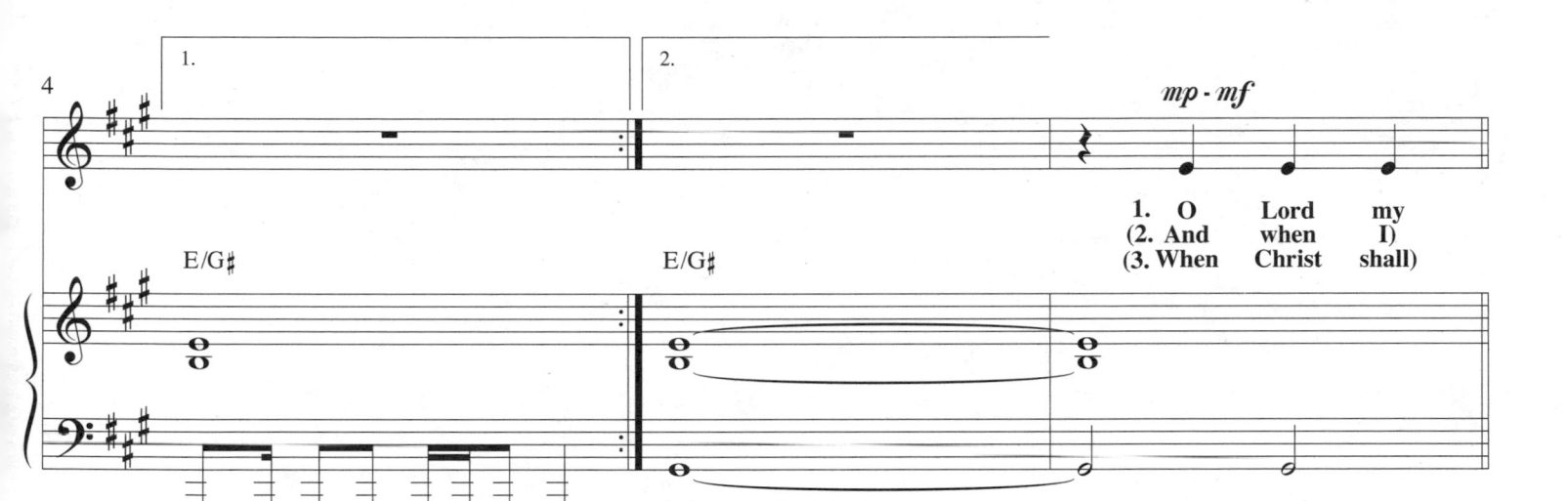

There Is A Fountain

Performed by Crystal Lewis

WILLIAM COWPER

TRADITIONAL AMERICAN MELODY

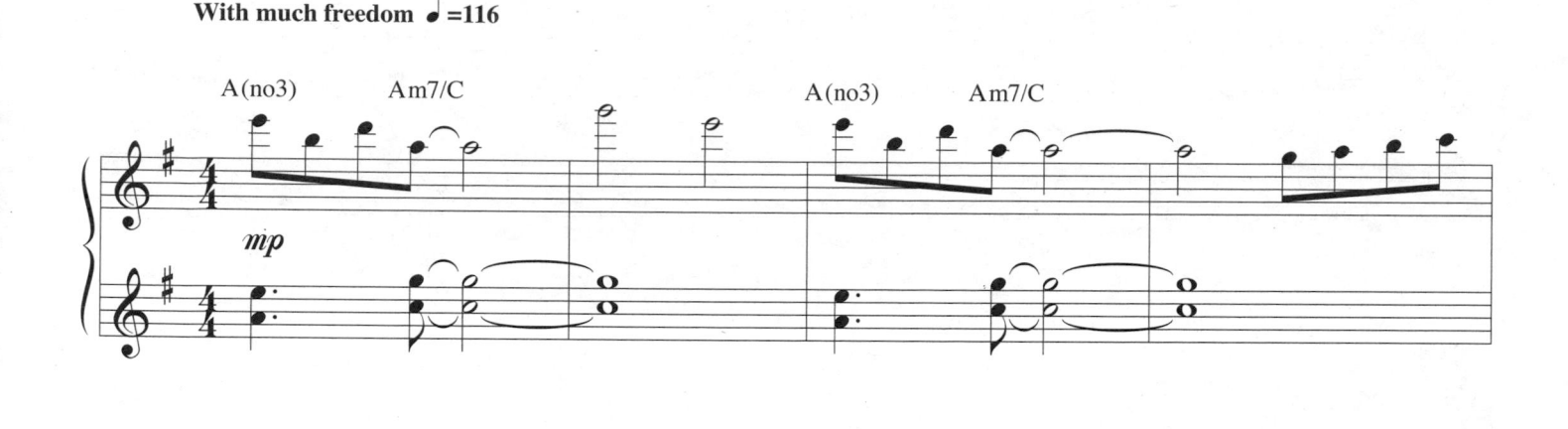

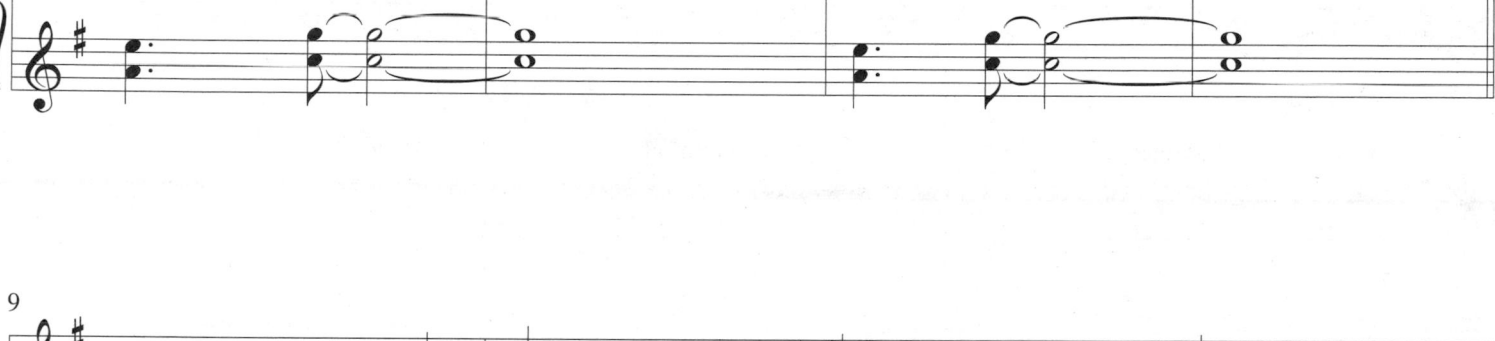

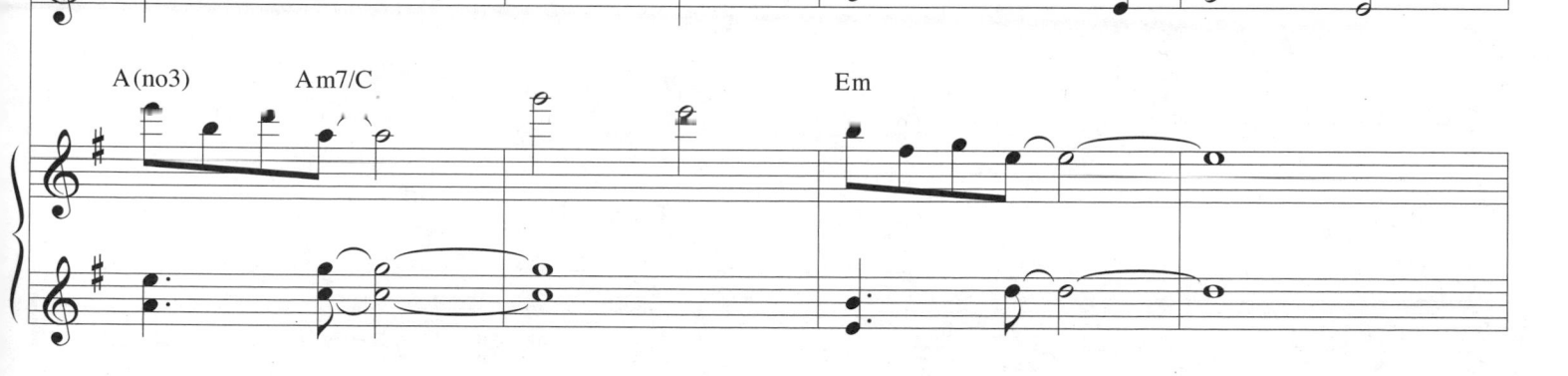

62
he, Wash all my sins a - way.
Am9 D7sus D7 G F/G G
66
Wash all my sins a - way, Wash
Bm7 Am7
71
all my sins a - way; And
G Fmaj9/G E♭maj7 D♭maj7 E♭2(no3)
75
there may I, though vile as he, Wash
G(no3) F/G G(no3) C9

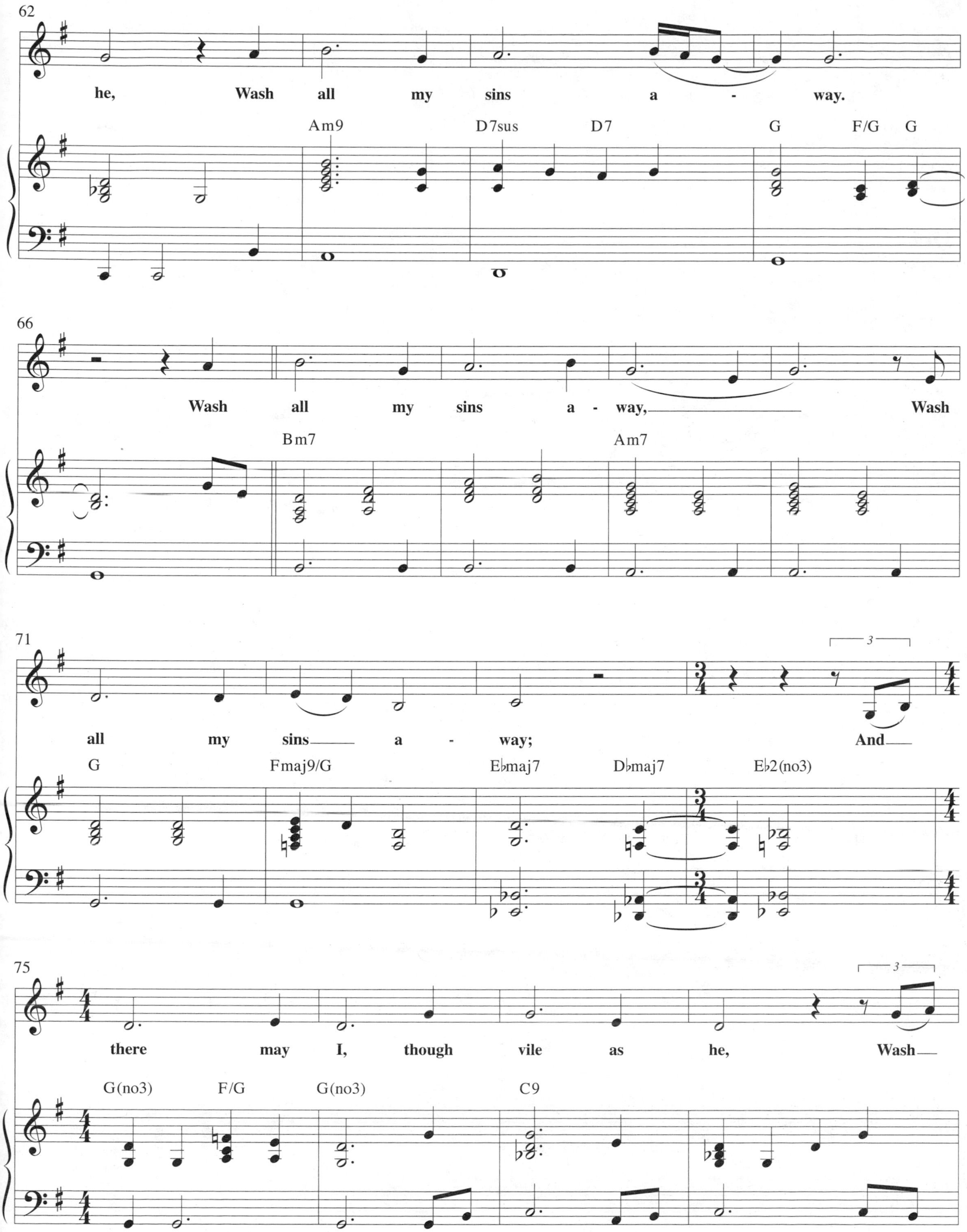

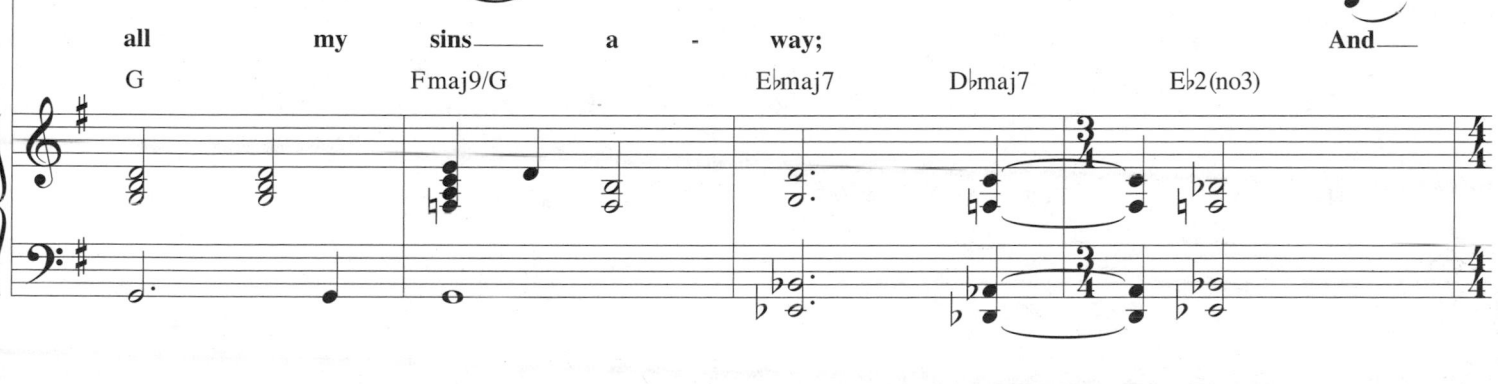

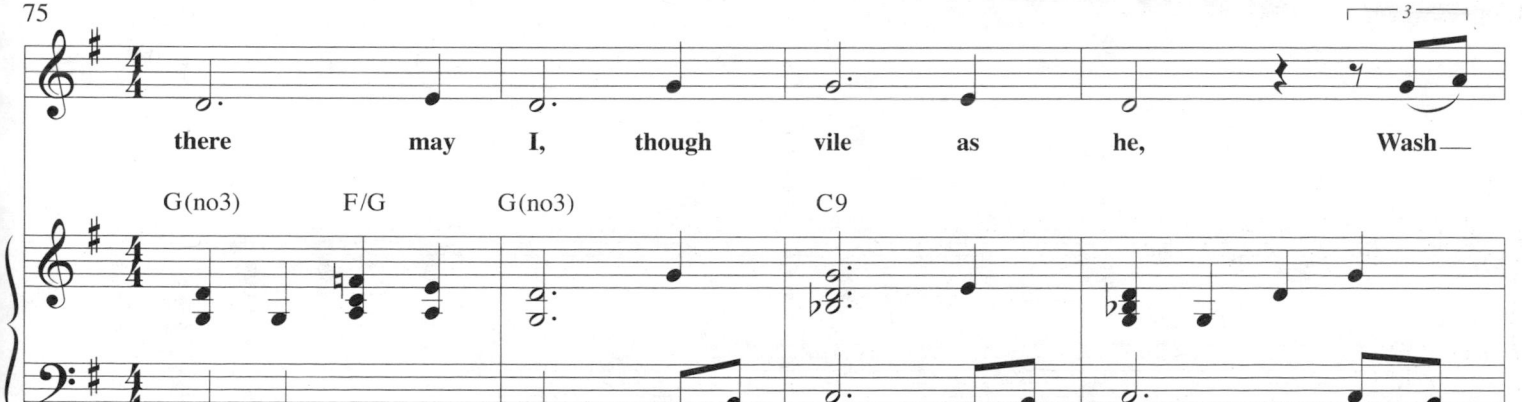

64

79

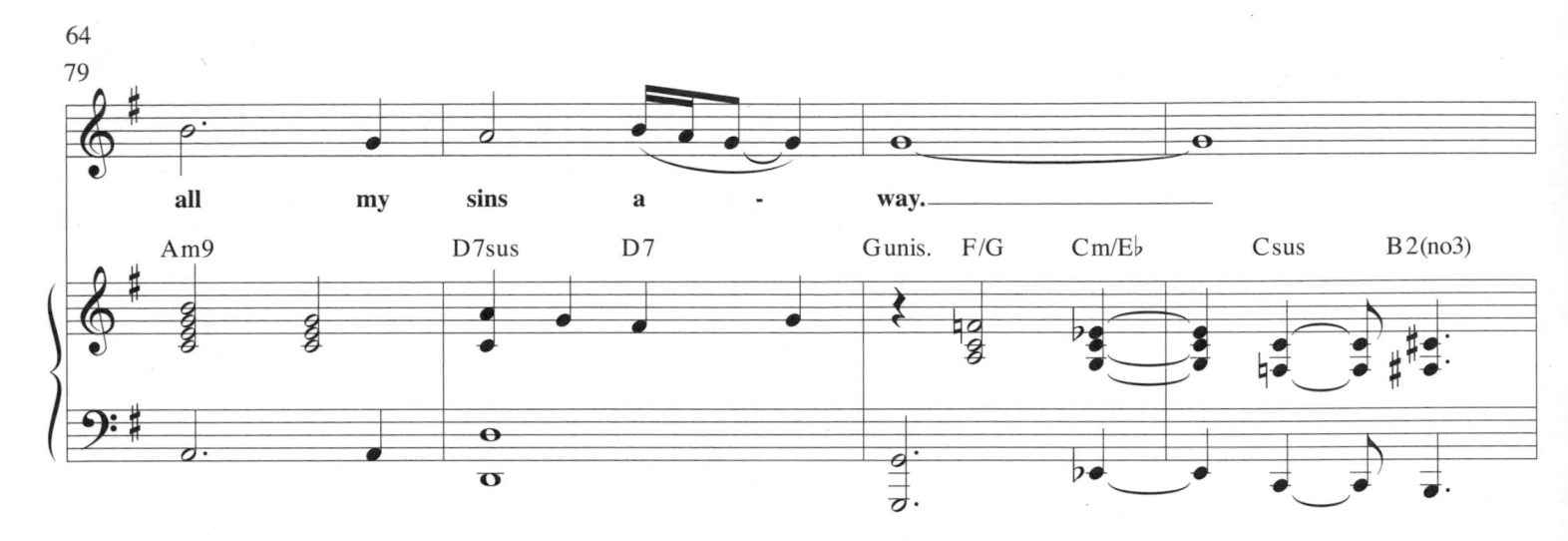

all   my   sins   a -   way.

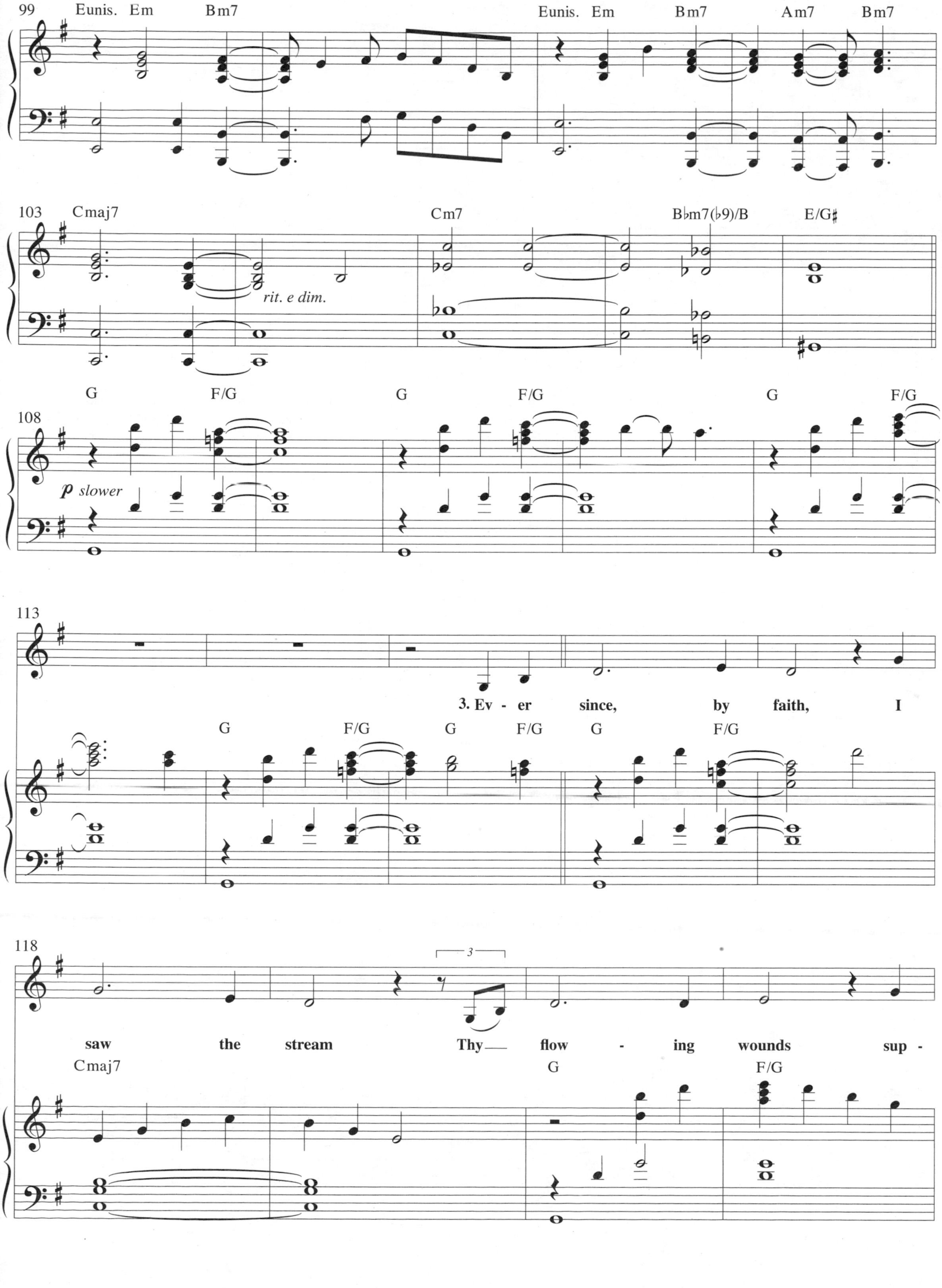

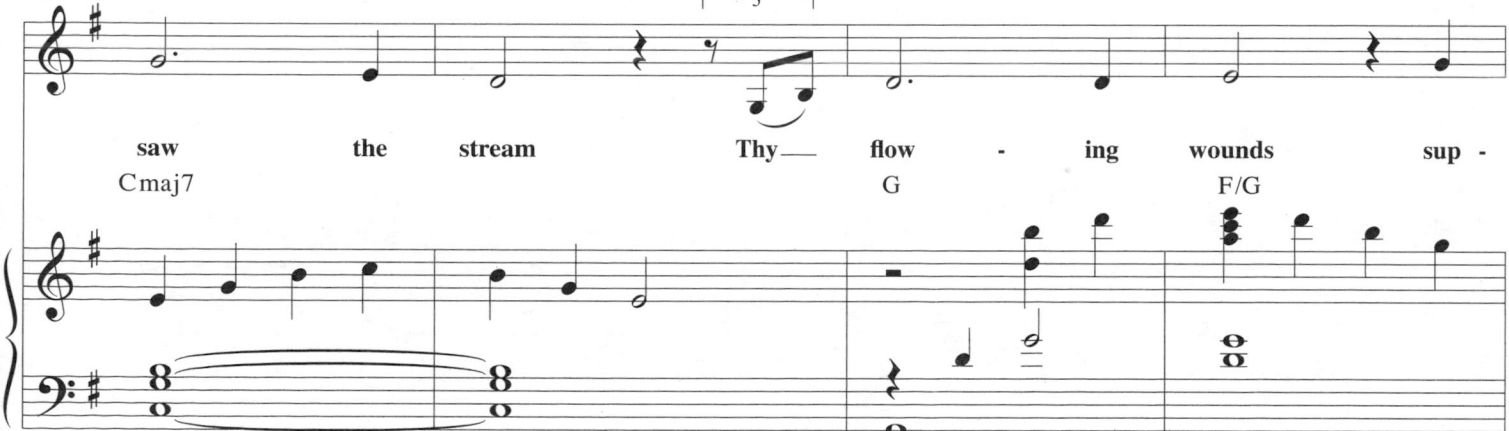

99
Eunis. Em
Bm7
Eunis. Em
Bm7
Am7
Bm7
103
Cmaj7
rit. e dim.
Cm7
B♭m7(♭9)/B
E/G♯
108
G
F/G
G
F/G
G
F/G
p slower
113
3. Ev - er since, by faith, I
G
F/G
G
F/G
G
F/G
118
saw the stream Thy flow - ing wounds sup -
Cmaj7
G
F/G

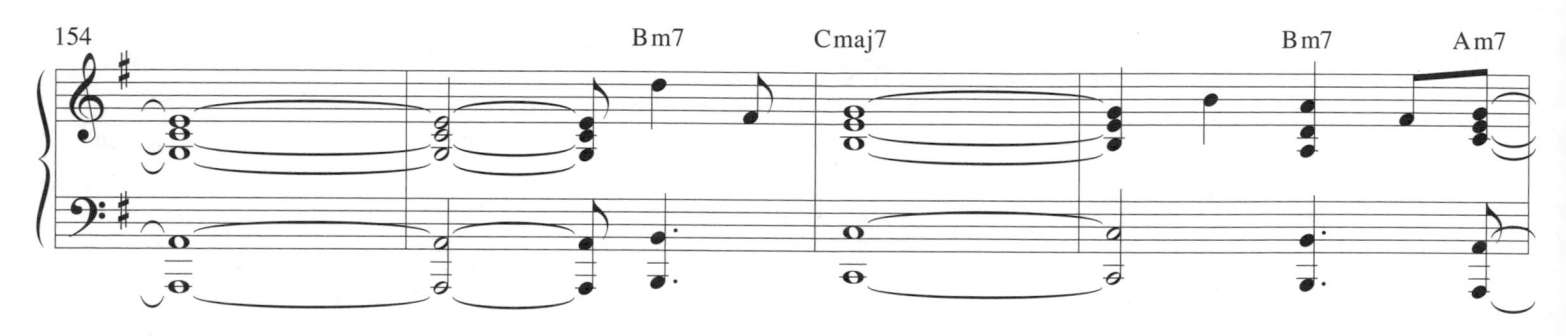

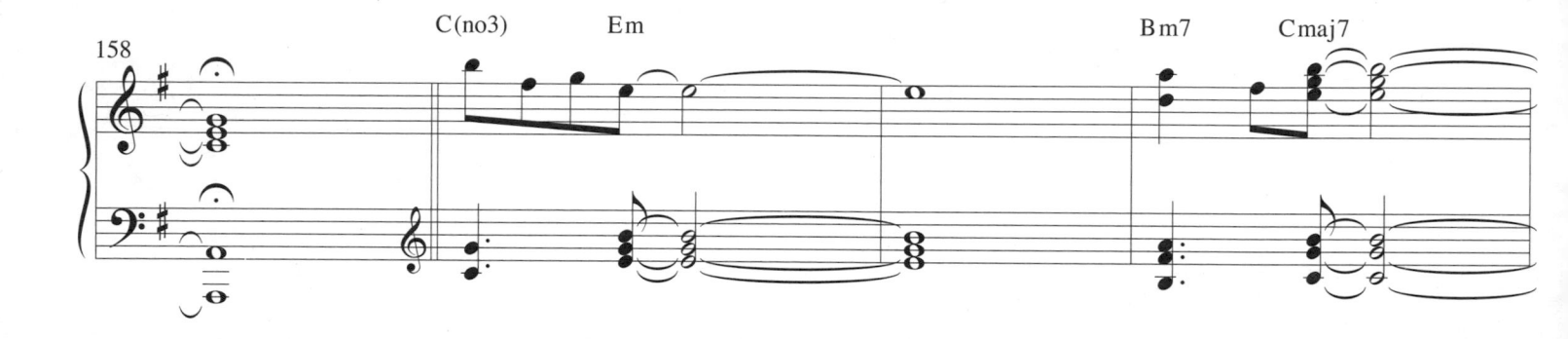

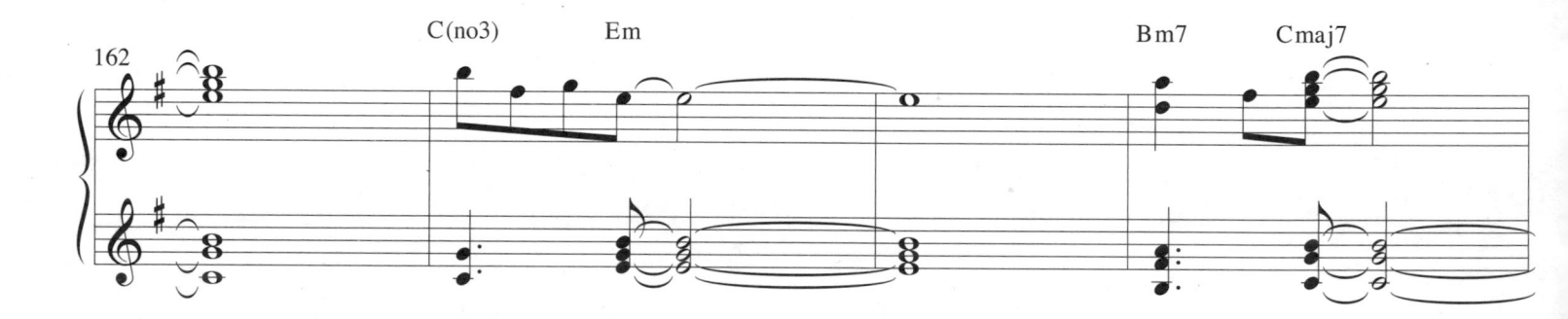

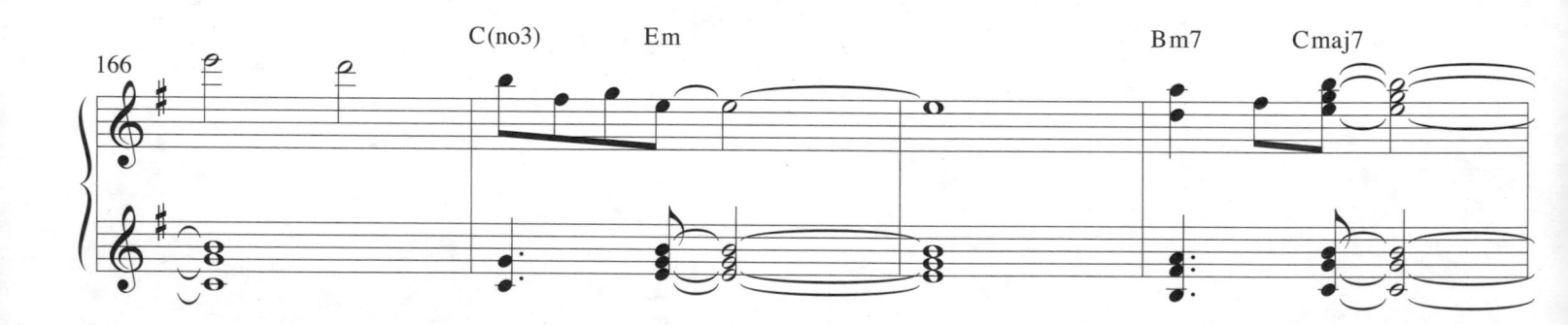

Because He Lives

Performed by Kristin Chenoweth

**GLORIA GAITHER
and WILLIAM J. GAITHER**

WILLIAM J. GAITHER

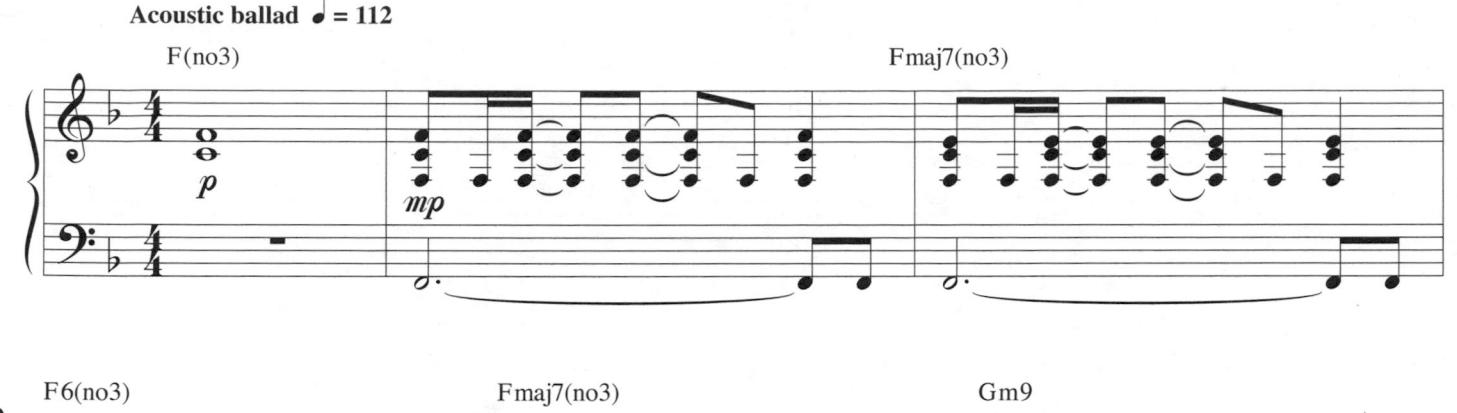

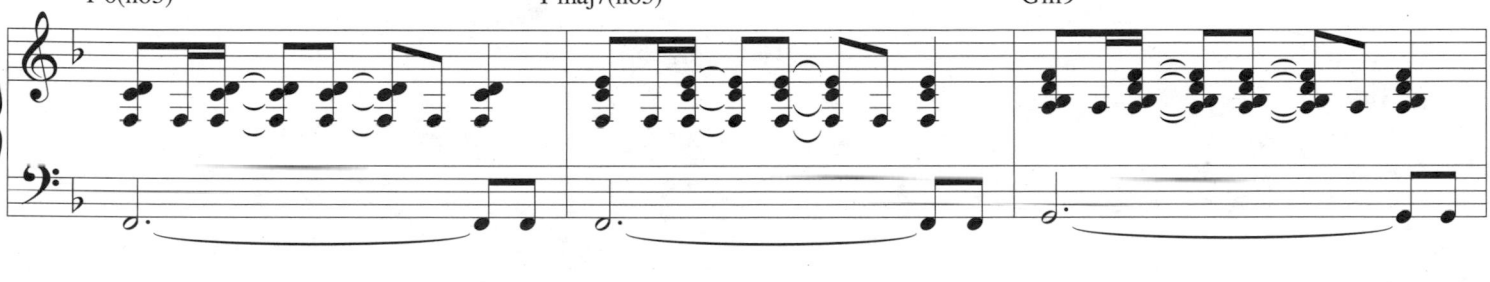

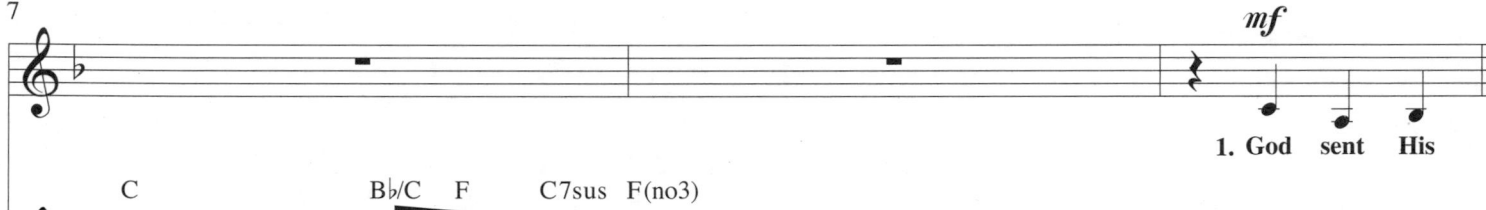

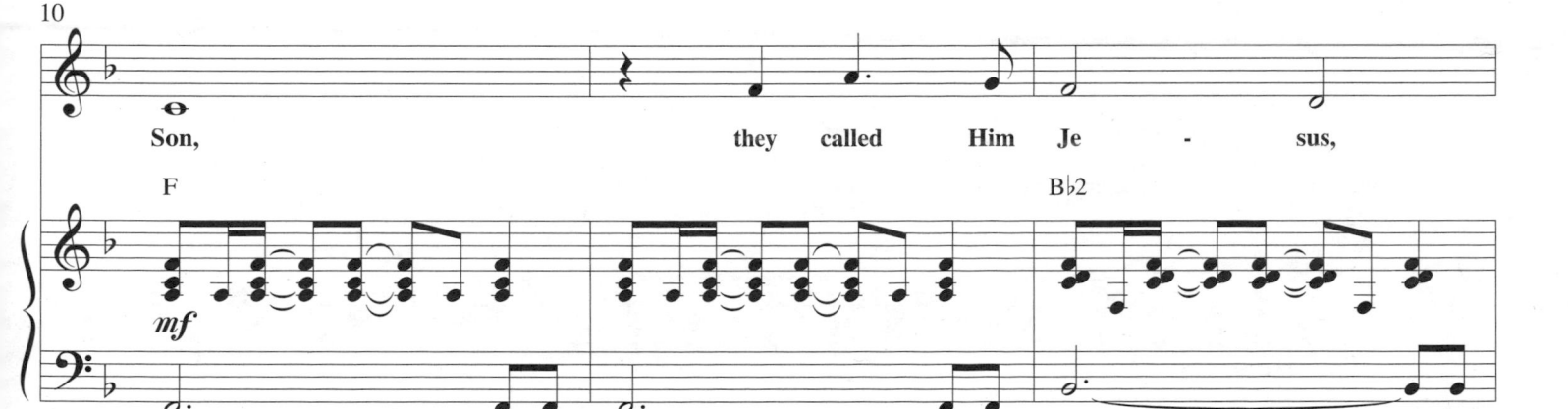

He came to love, heal, and for -

give; He lived and died

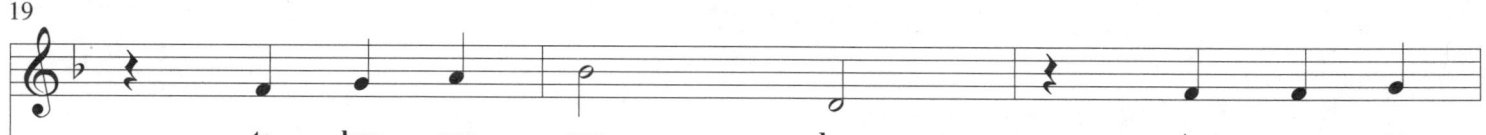

to buy my par - don, An emp - ty

grave is there to prove my Sav - ior lives.

36

2nd time to CODA

fu - ture.   And life is worth the liv - ing

B♭2   F

39

just   be - cause   He   lives.   2. How sweet to

C   B♭   Gm7(4)

42

hold   a   new - born——— ba - by,———

F   Fsus

45

And feel—— the   pride,   and joy—— he

F

What A Friend We Have In Jesus

Performed by Paul Baloche

JOSEPH M. SCRIVEN

CHARLES C. CONVERSE

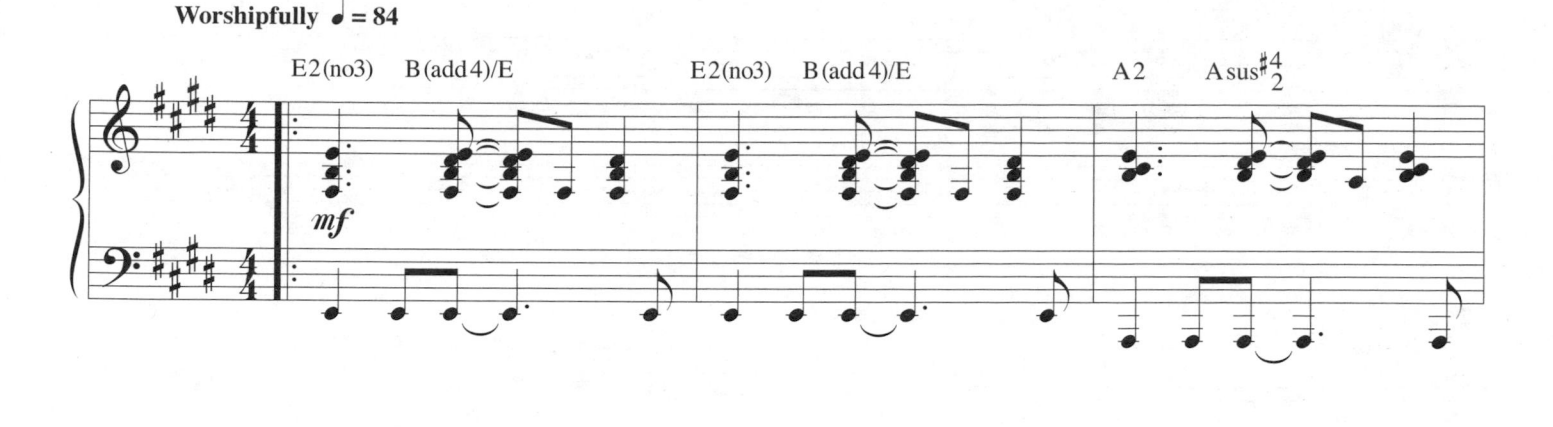

1. What a friend we have in Je - sus,
2. Have we tri - als and temp - ta - tions?

all our sins and griefs to bear!
Is there trou - ble an - y - where?

2. O

prayer.

Are we weak and heav-y lad - en, Cum - bered with a load of

care?   Pre - cious Sav - ior, still— our ref - uge;

Take My Life, And Let It Be Consecrated

Performed by Leann Albrecht

FRANCES RIDLEY HAVERGAL

HENRI A. CESAR MALAN

Acoustic folk ♩ = 96

2nd time only: opt. accordian cues

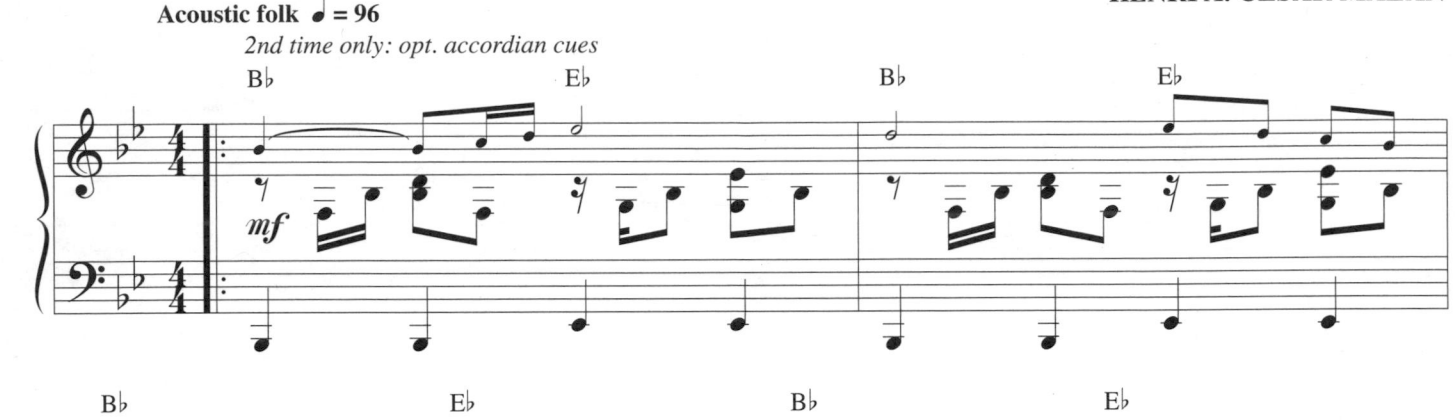

1. Take my life and let it be con-se-crat-ed, Lord, to Thee; Take my mo-ments and my days—

I Surrender All

Performed by Israel Houghton

JUDSON W. VAN DeVENTER

WINFIELD S. WEEDEN

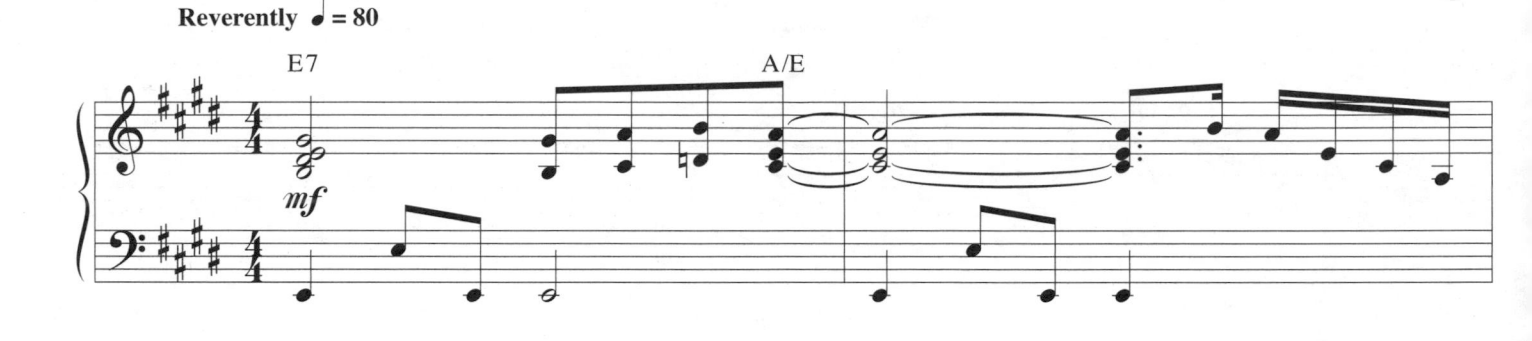

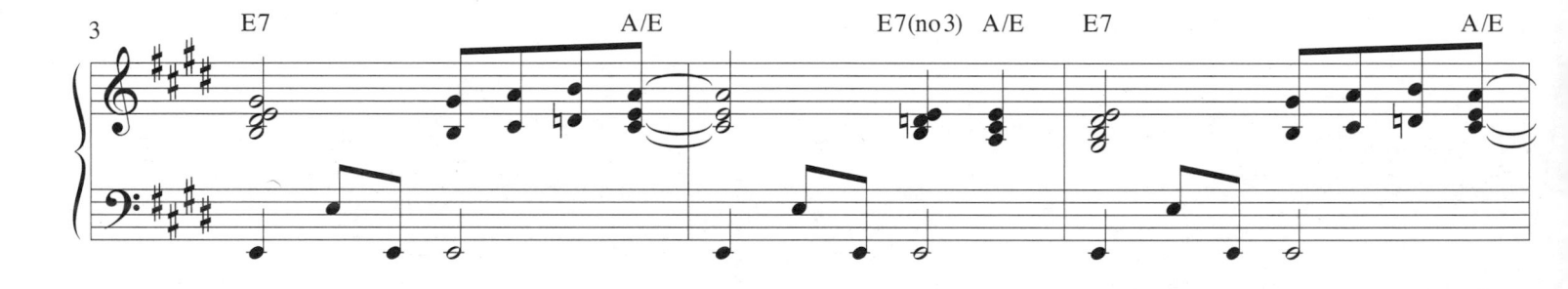

All_____ to Je - sus I_____ sur - ren - der,_____ All to Him I

36
All to Je - sus I sur - ren - der, Make me, Sav - ior,
E   A/E   E   B/D#   G#   G#7   C#m   F#m7   E/G#

39
whol - ly thine; Let me feel Thy Ho - ly Spir - it,
F#m/B   B7(6)   E   A/E   E   A/E   E   B/D#   G#   G#7

42
D.S. al CODA 𝄋
Tru - ly know that thou art_____ mine.
C#m   F#m7   E/G#   F#m/B   B7(6)   E   A/E

𝄉 **CODA**

44
all.   All   to   Je - sus   I   sur - ren - der,
E   A/E   E   B/D#   G#   G#7/B#

All Hail The Power Of Jesus' Name

Performed by the Maranatha! Singers

OLIVER HOLDEN

EDWARD PERRONET, stanzas 1, 2
JOHN RIPPON, stanza 3

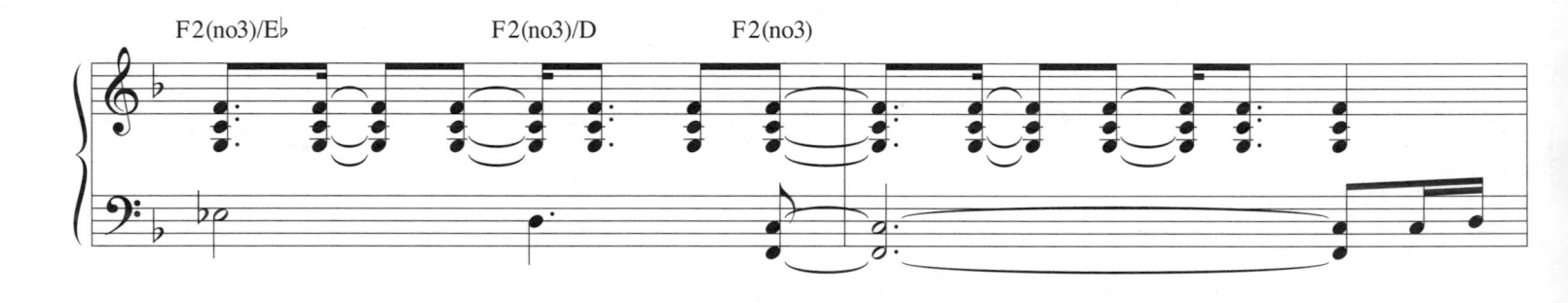

1. All hail the pow'r of

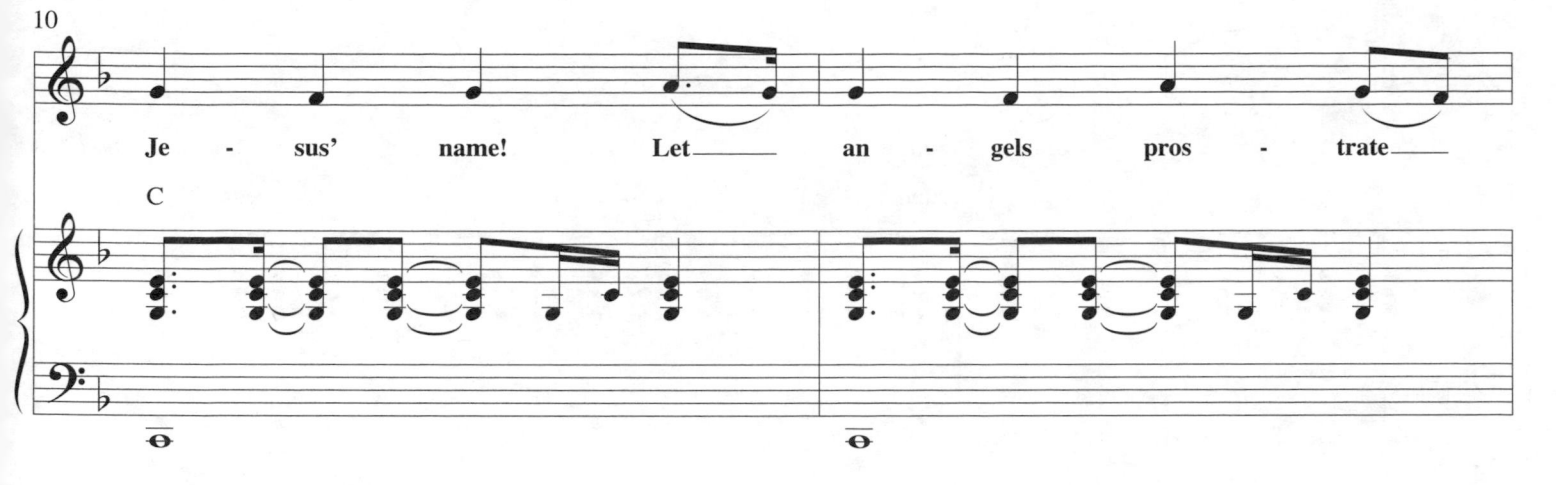

Je - sus' name! Let_____ an - gels pros - trate_____

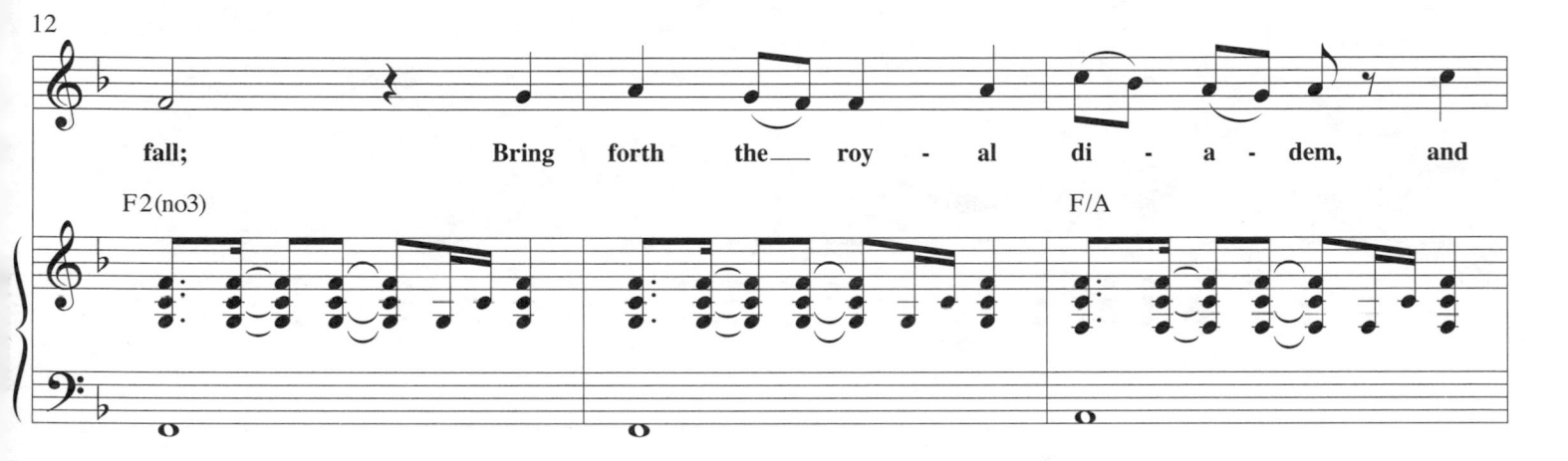

fall; Bring forth the_____ roy - al di - a - dem, and

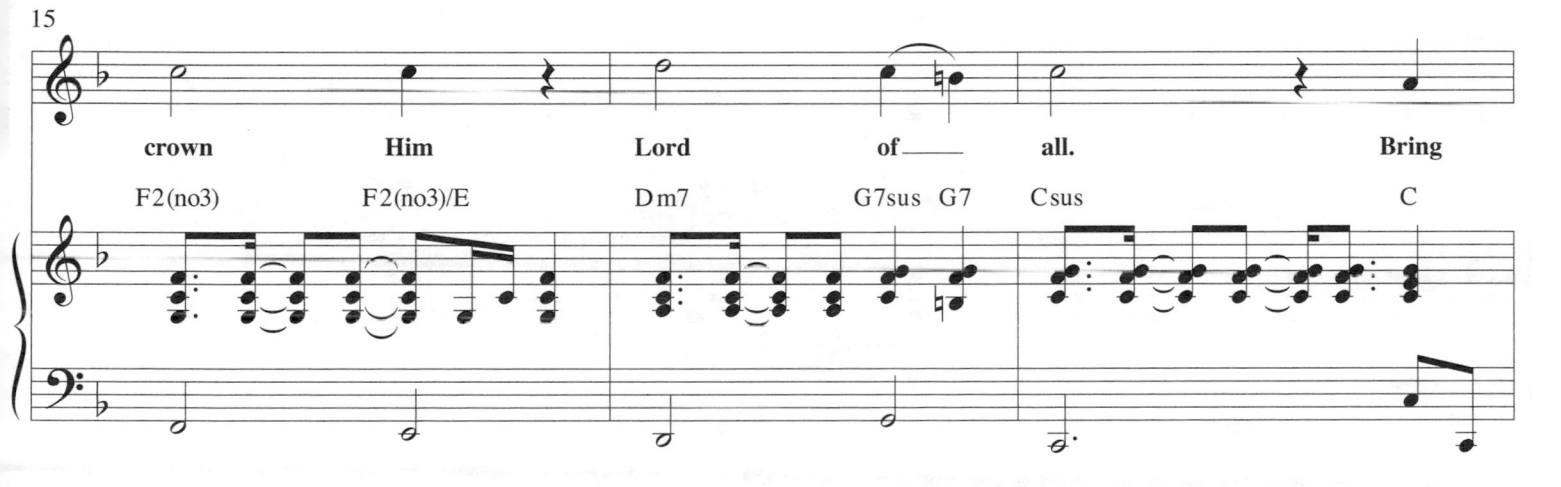

crown Him Lord of_____ all. Bring

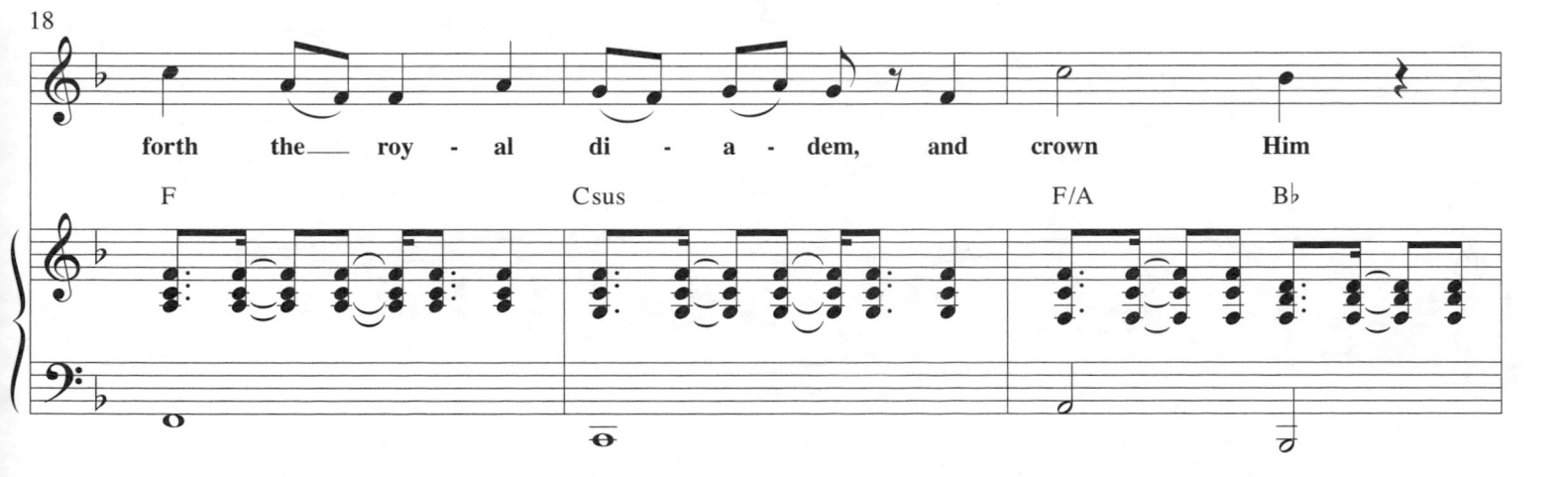

forth the_____ roy - al di - a - dem, and crown Him

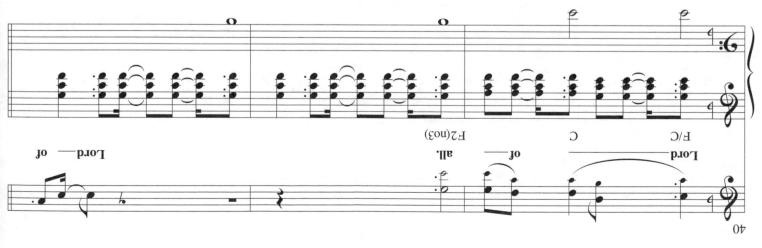

Him all maj - es - ty____ as - cribe, And

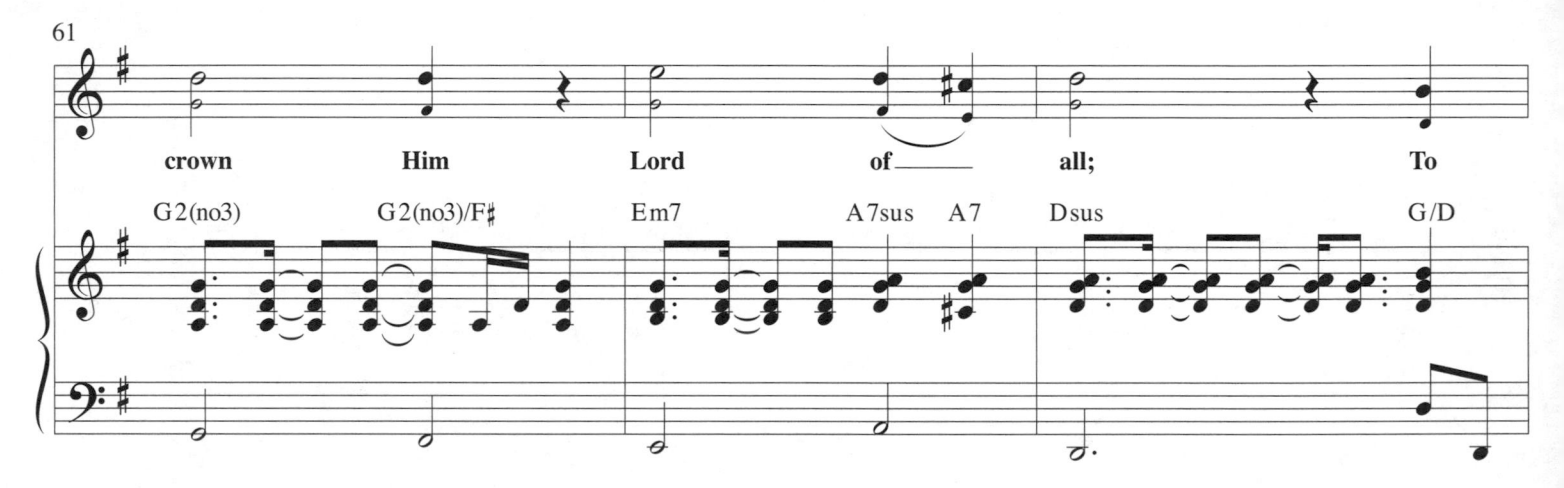

crown Him Lord of____ all; To

Him all maj - es - ty____ as - cribe, And

crown Him Lord_____ of____

'Cause He's wor - thy of____ our praise.____

Crown   Him,   Lord_____   of____

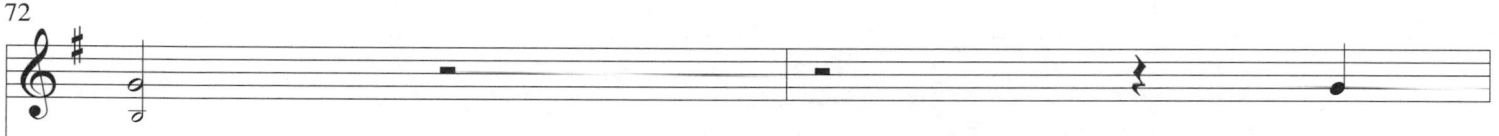

all.   And

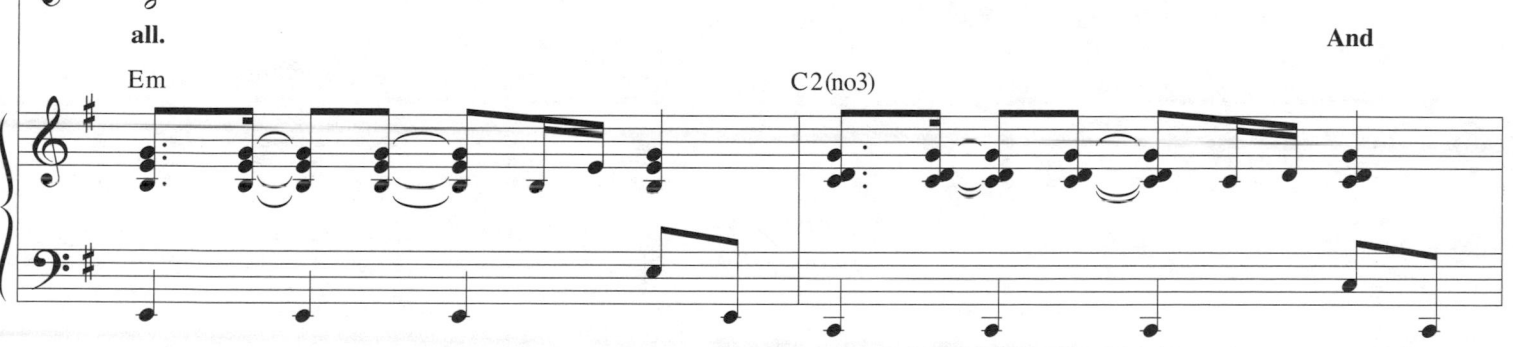

crown   Him   Lord_____   of__ all.

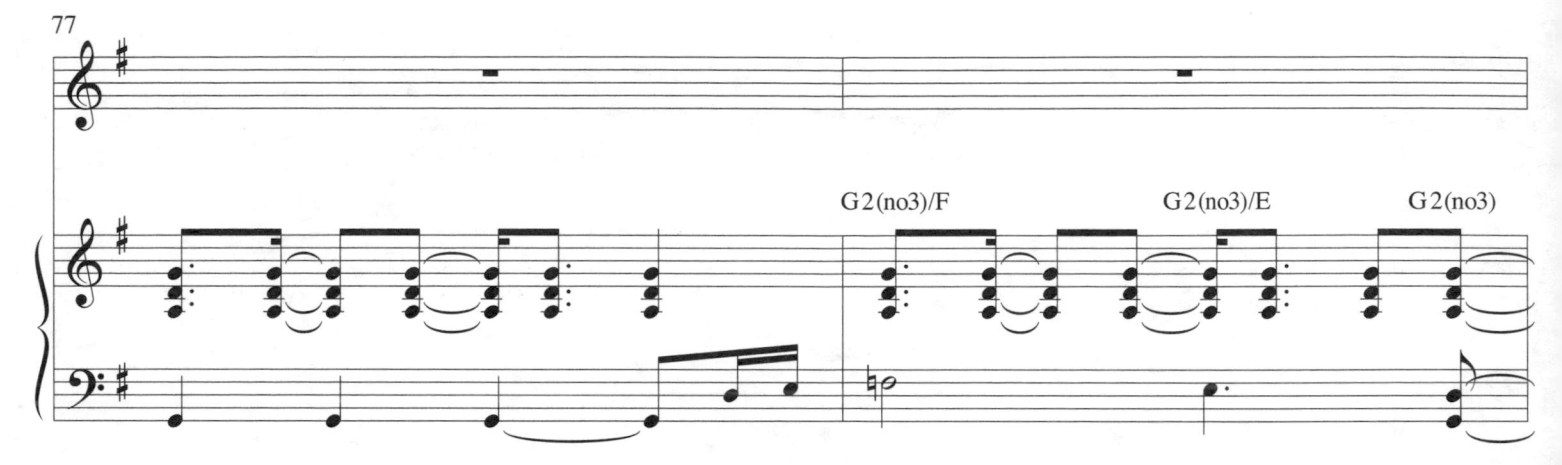

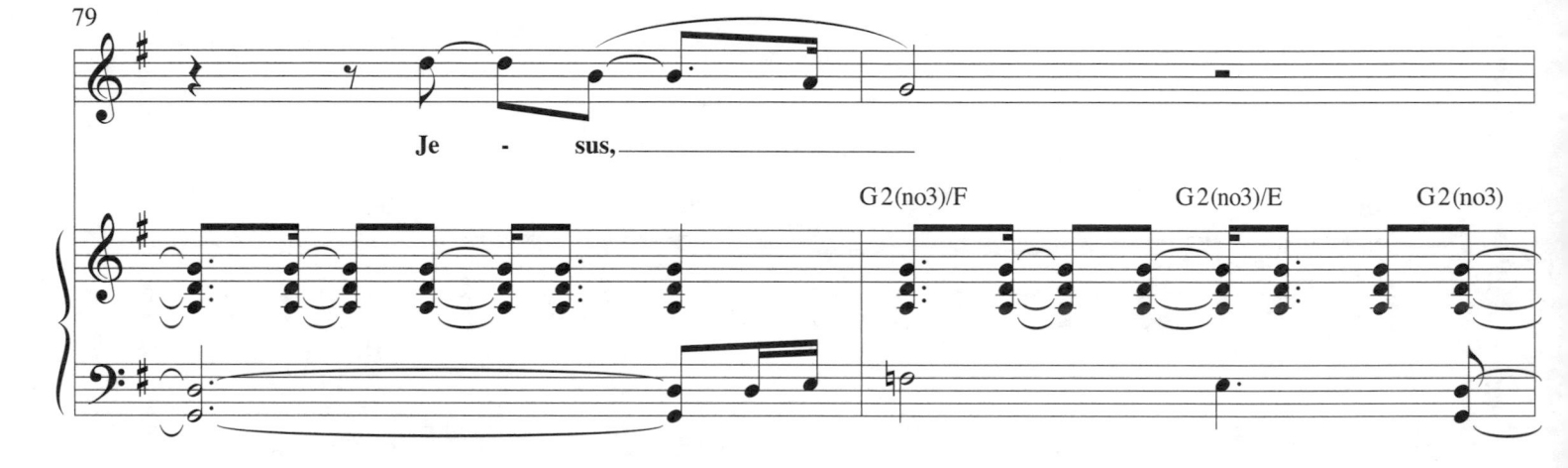

Here Is Love Vast As The Ocean

Performed by Sheila Walsh

Words and Music by
UNKNOWN
Arranged by John Hartley,
Adam DePasquale and Jared DePasquale

Amazing Grace

Performed by Darlene Zschech

JOHN NEWTON

TRADITIONAL AMERICAN MELODY
From Carreel and Clayton's *Virginia Harmony, 1831*
Arranged by Darlene Zschech

With freedom ♩ = 100

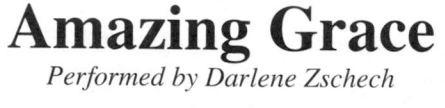

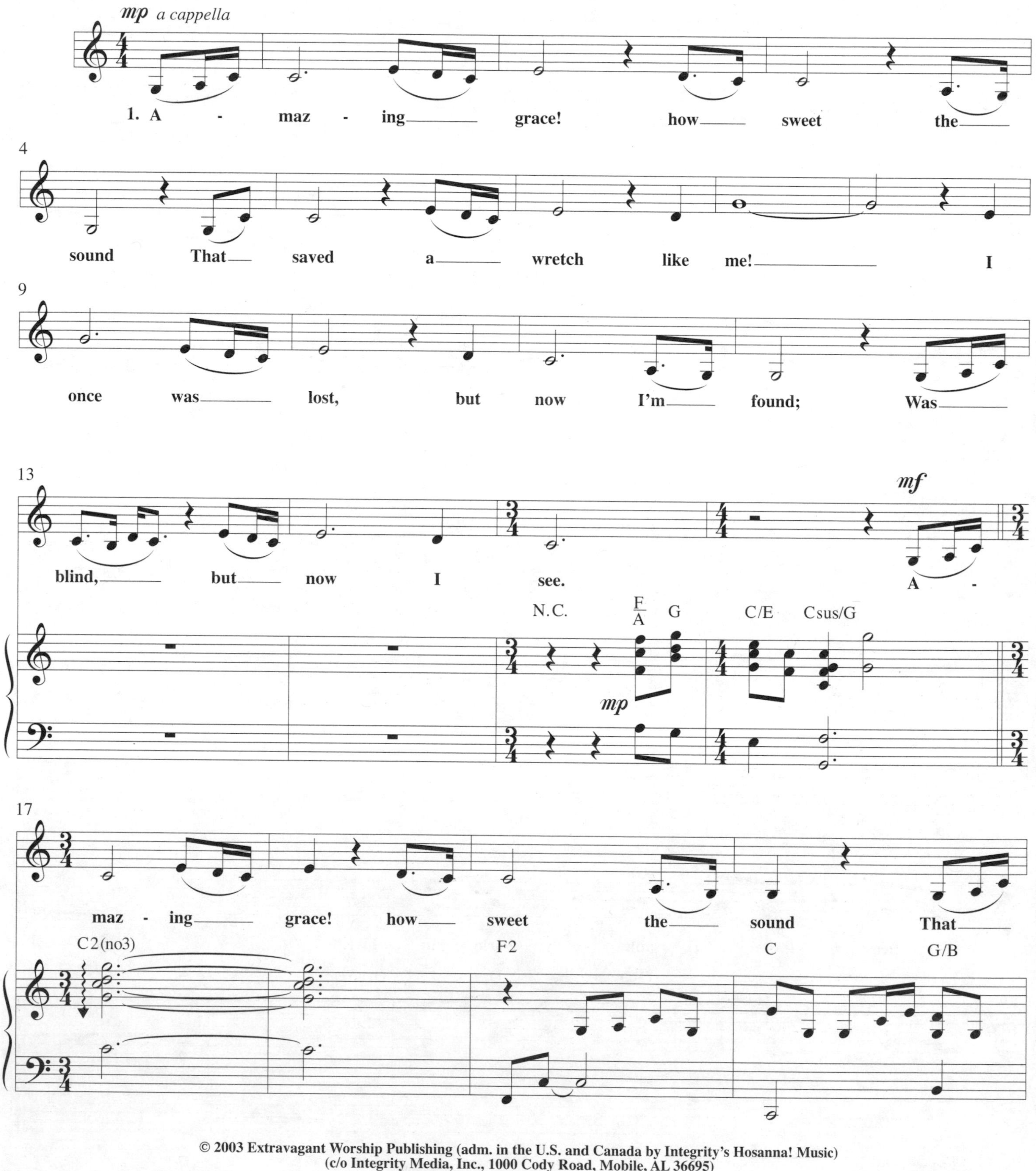
mp a cappella
1. A - maz - ing grace! how sweet the
4
sound That saved a wretch like me! I
9
once was lost, but now I'm found; Was
13
mf
blind, but now I see. A -
N.C.
F/A
G
C/E
Csus/G
mp
17
maz - ing grace! how sweet the sound That
C2(no3)
F2
C
G/B

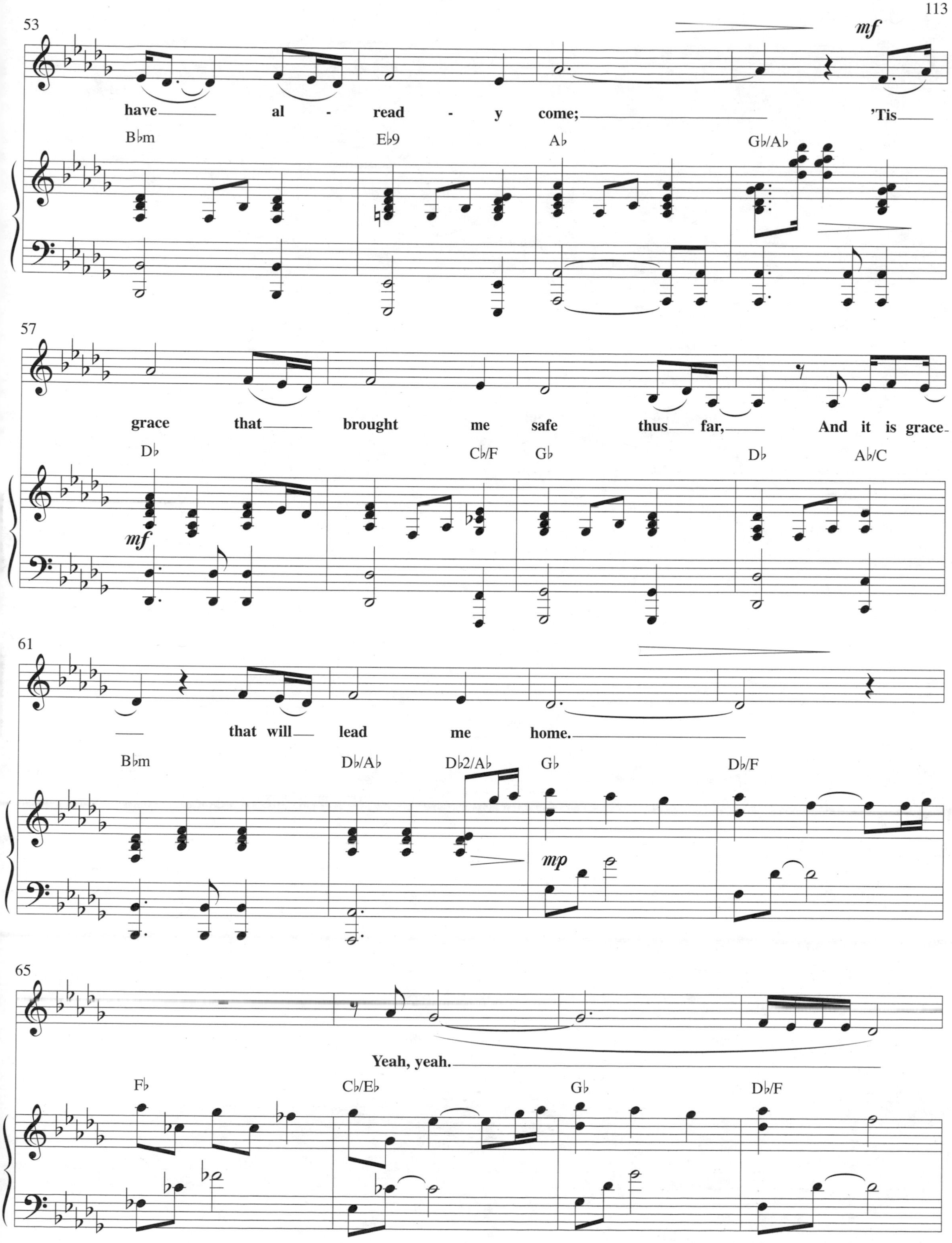
53
mf
have al - read - y come; 'Tis
B♭m E♭9 A♭ G♭/A♭
57
grace that brought me safe thus far, And it is grace
D♭ C♭/F G♭ D♭ A♭/C
mf
61
that will lead me home.
B♭m D♭/A♭ D♭2/A♭ G♭ D♭/F
mp
65
Yeah, yeah.
F♭ C♭/E♭ G♭ D♭/F

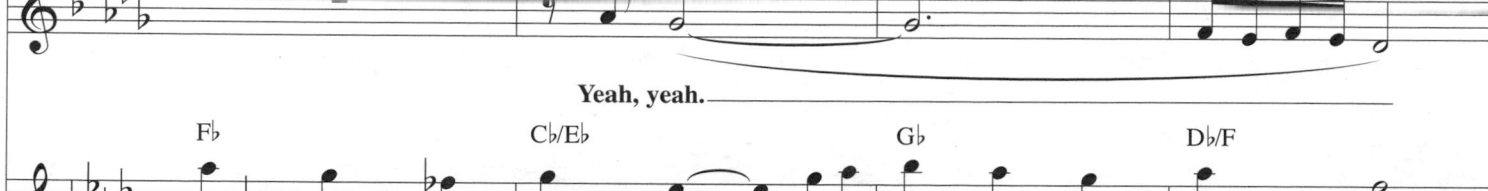

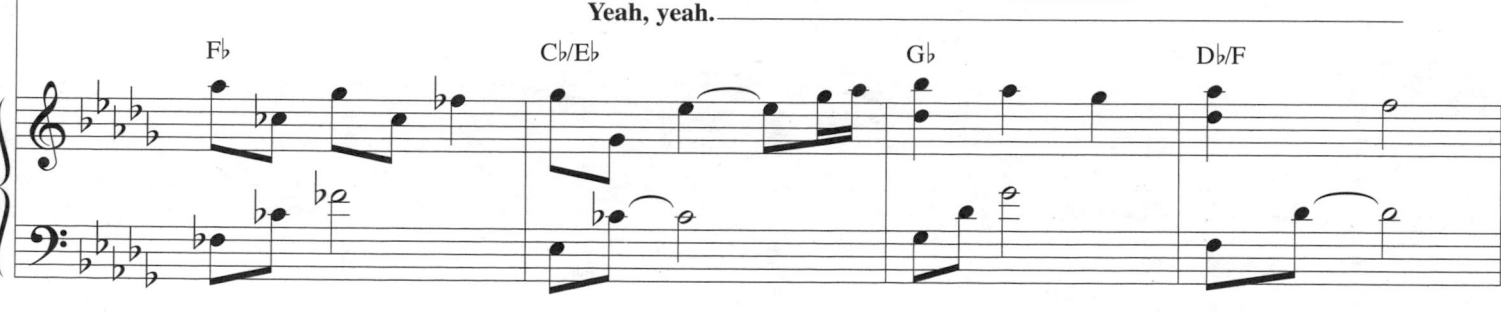

It Is Well With My Soul

Performed by 4Him

HORATIO G. SPAFFORD

PHILIP P. BLISS
Arranged by Paul Mills and Wayne Watson

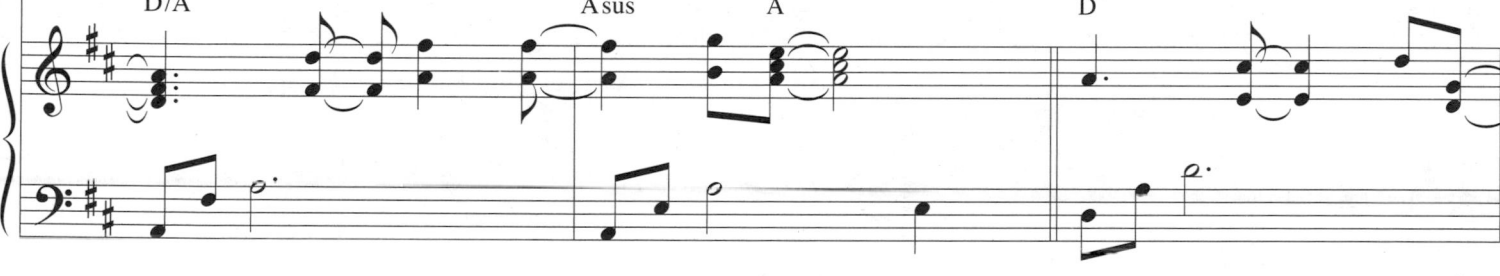

Oh yeah. 2. Though Sa - tan____ should

buf - fet,____ though tri - als____ should come,____ Let

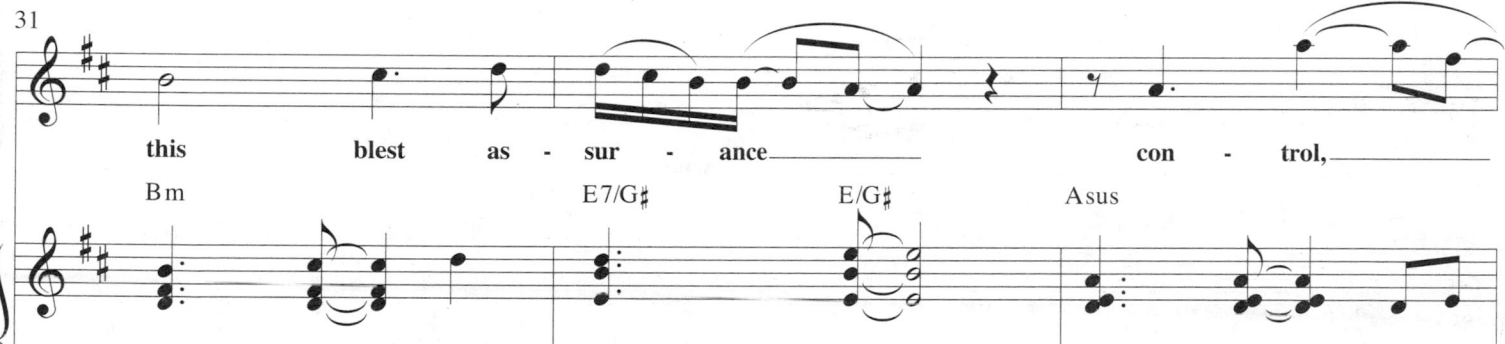

this blest as - sur - ance____ con - trol,____

That Christ____ hath____ re - gard - ed____ my help -

3. My sin— oh, the bliss— of— this glo-

- ri - ous thought:— Oh,— my— sin not— in part,—

— but— the whole,— Is nailed—

to the cross and I bear it no more,

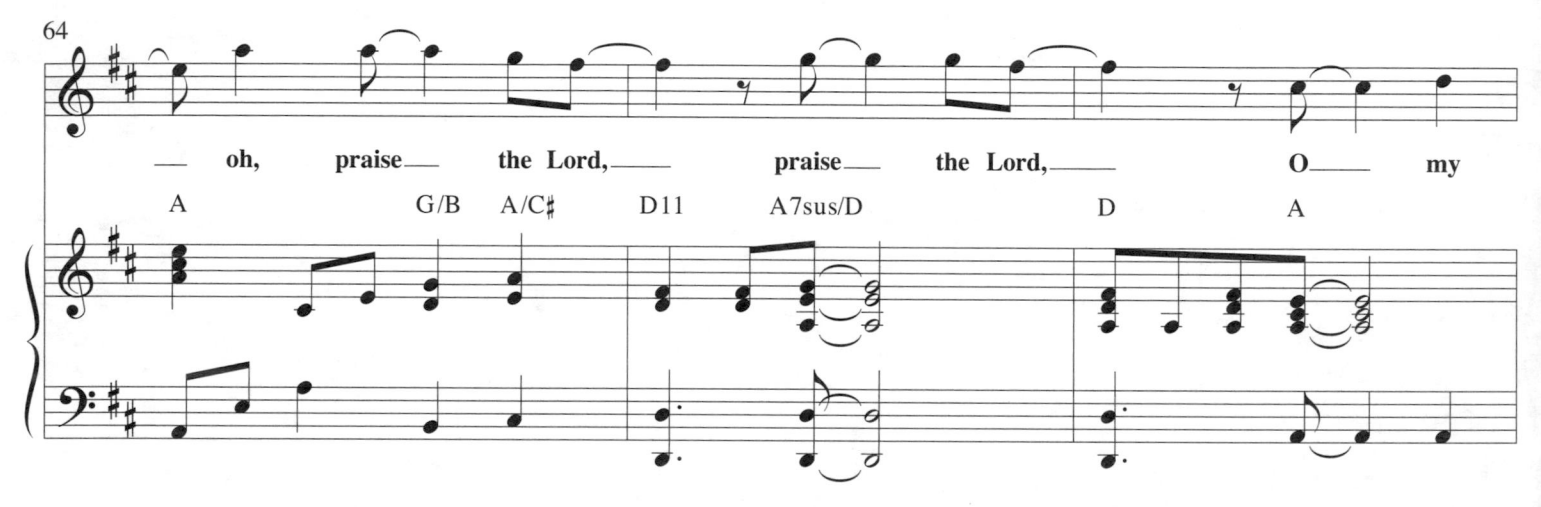

oh, praise the Lord, praise the Lord, O my

soul, O praise the Lord.

4. And, Lord, haste the day when my faith

shall— be sight,— The clouds— be— rolled back—

— as— a scroll:— The trump—

— shall— re-sound— and— the Lord— shall— de-scend,—

"E-ven so"— it— is well— with— my—

Blessed Assurance, Jesus Is Mine

Performed by Leann Albrecht and Bob Fitts

FANNY J. CROSBY

PHOEBE P. KNAPP

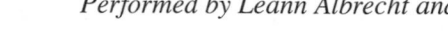

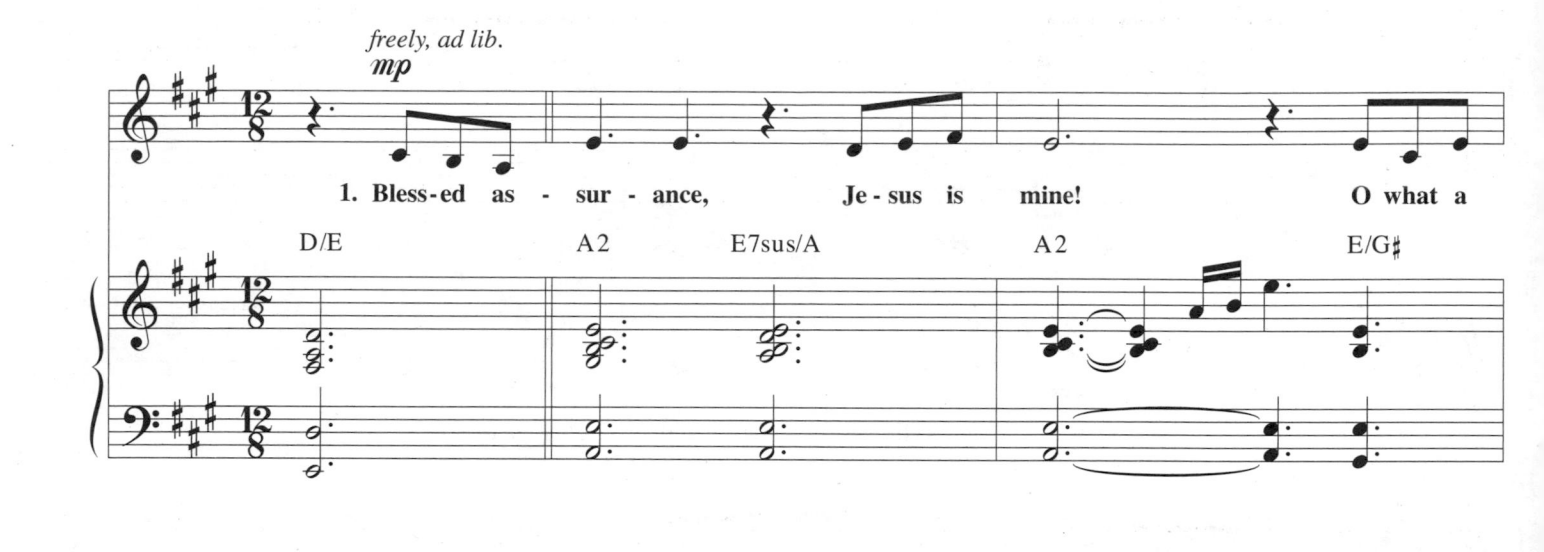

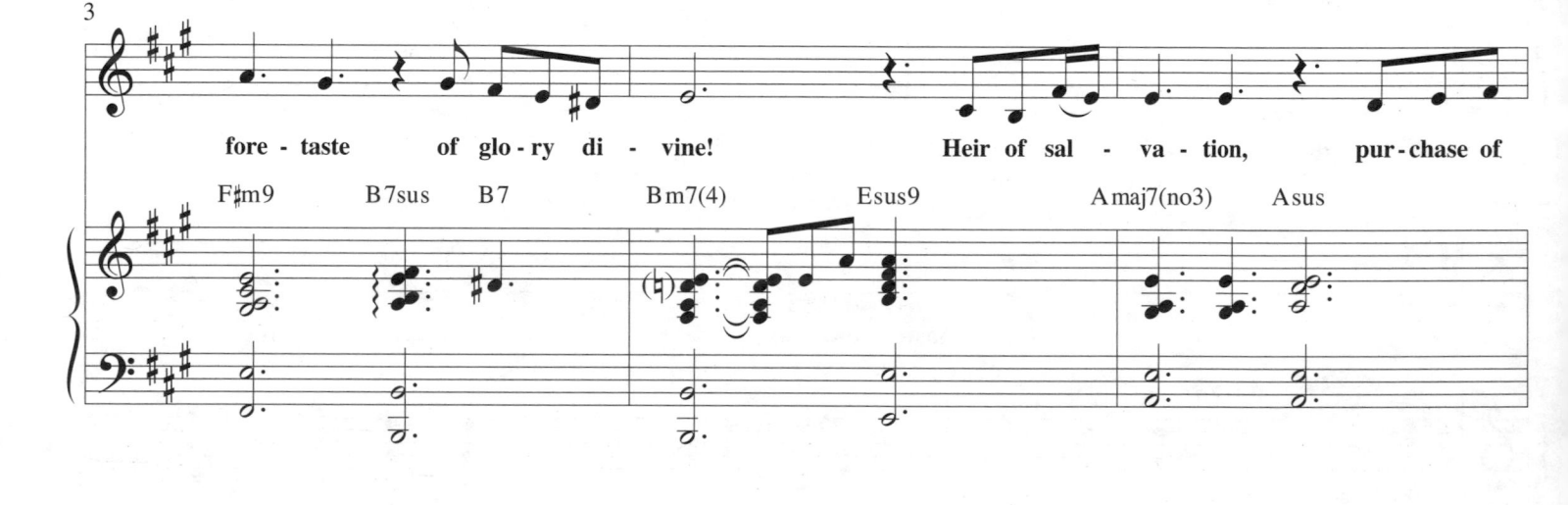

blood.

2. Per - fect sub - mis - sion, all is at
3. mis - sion, per - fect de -

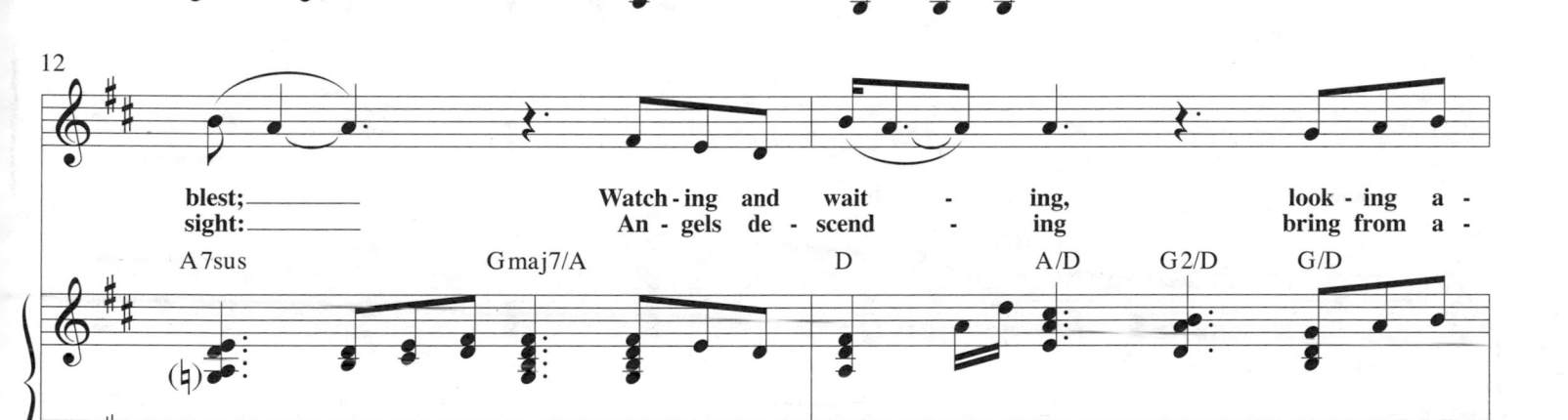

rest, I in my Sav - ior am hap - py and
light, Vi - sions of rap - ture now burst on my

blest;_____ Watch - ing and wait - ing, look - ing a -
sight:_____ An - gels de - scend - ing bring from a -

bove, Filled with His good - ness, lost in His
bove, Ech - oes of mer - cy, whis - pers of

Pass Me Not, O Gentle Savior

Performed by Fernando Ortega

FANNY J. CROSBY

WILLIAM H. DOANE
Arranged by John Andrew Schreiner

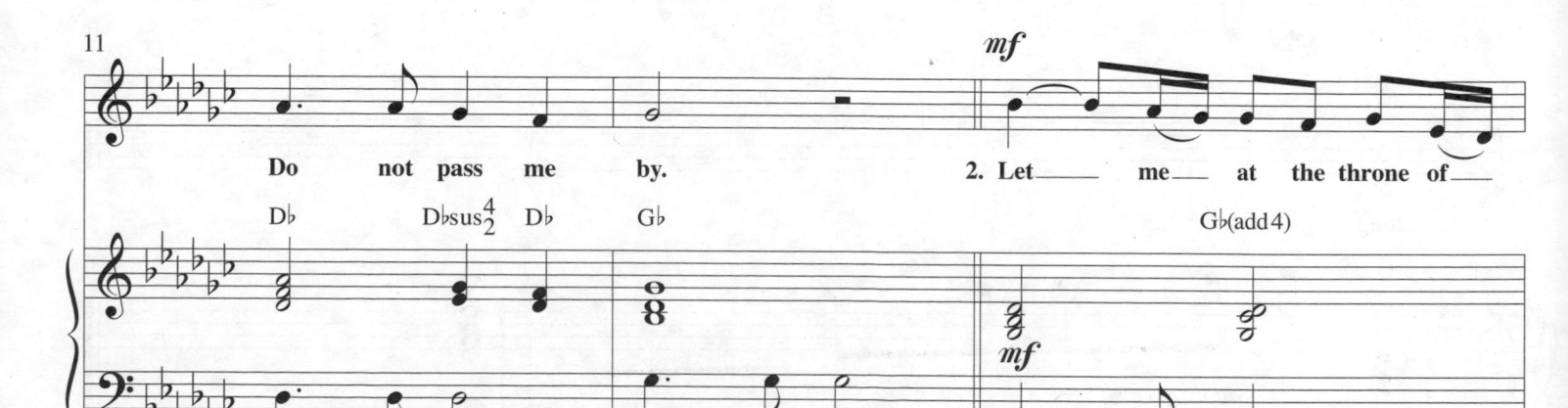

14
mer - cy Find a sweet re - lief;
G♭2 G♭ D♭/F E♭m2 E♭m C♭maj7
17
Kneel - ing there in deep con - tri - tion, Help my un - be -
G♭2 G♭sus G♭ E♭m2 E♭m A♭m C♭/D♭ D♭9
20
lief. Sav - ior, Sav - ior, Hear my hum-ble cry;
G♭sus G♭ A♭m/G♭ G♭ E♭m7 A♭7sus/D♭ D♭
25
While on oth-ers Thou art call - ing, Do not pass me by.
E♭m2 C♭2 B♭m7 E♭m2 E♭m A♭ G♭/D♭ D♭ G♭

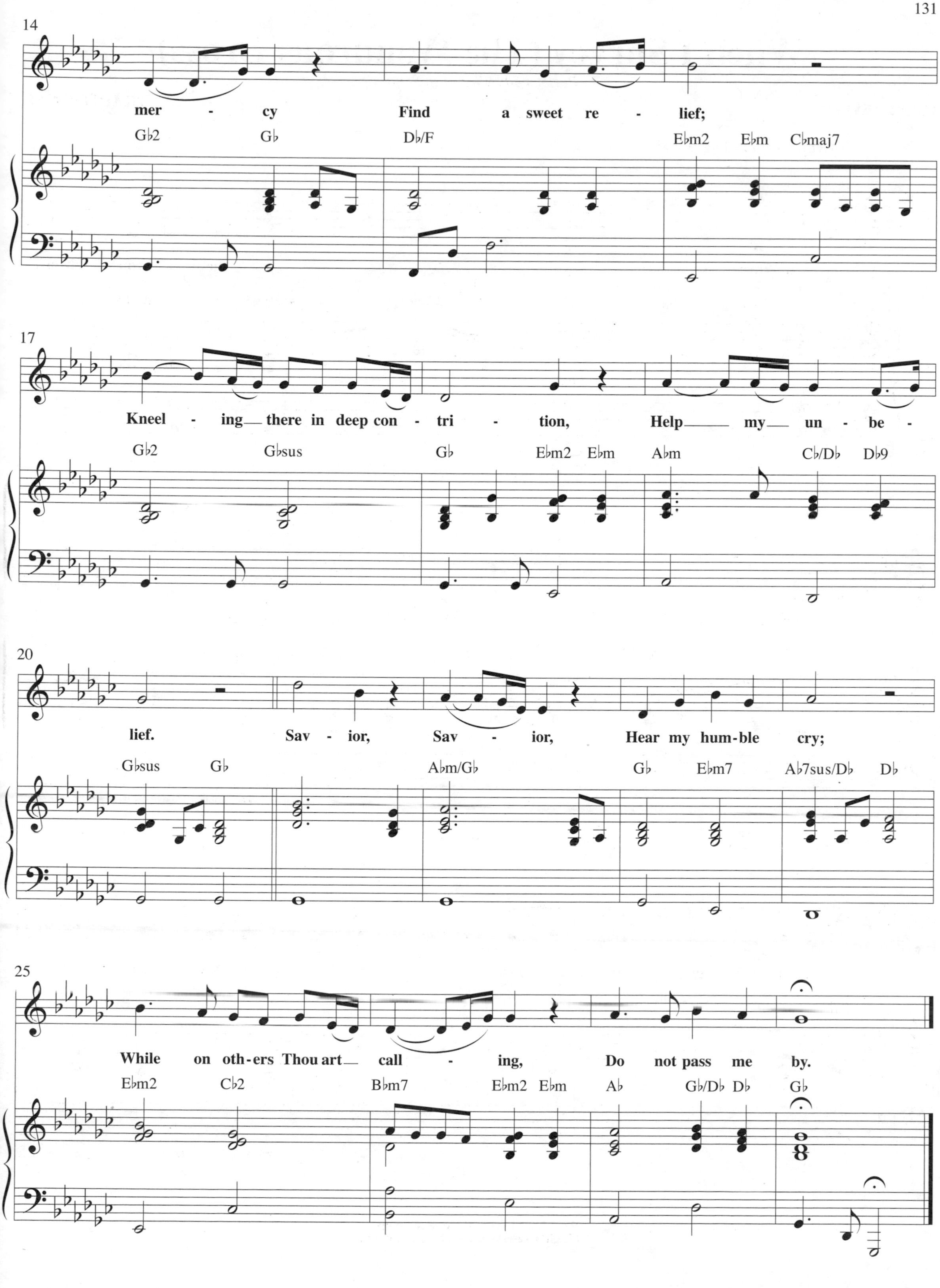

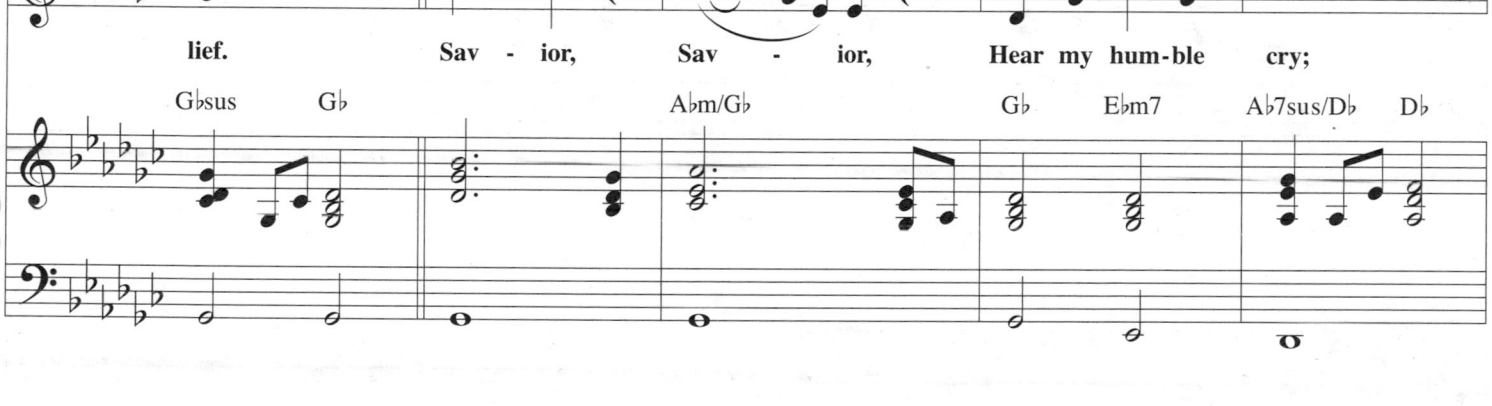

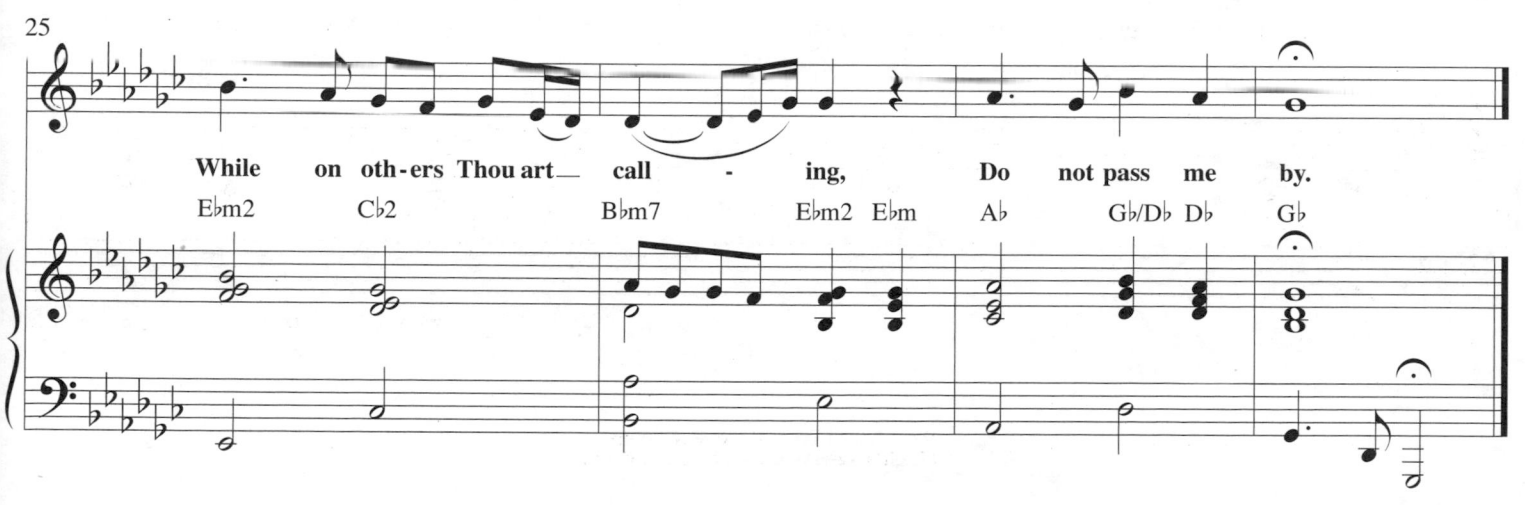

When I Survey (The Wondrous Cross)

Performed by Kathryn Scott

ISAAC WATTS

TRADITIONAL

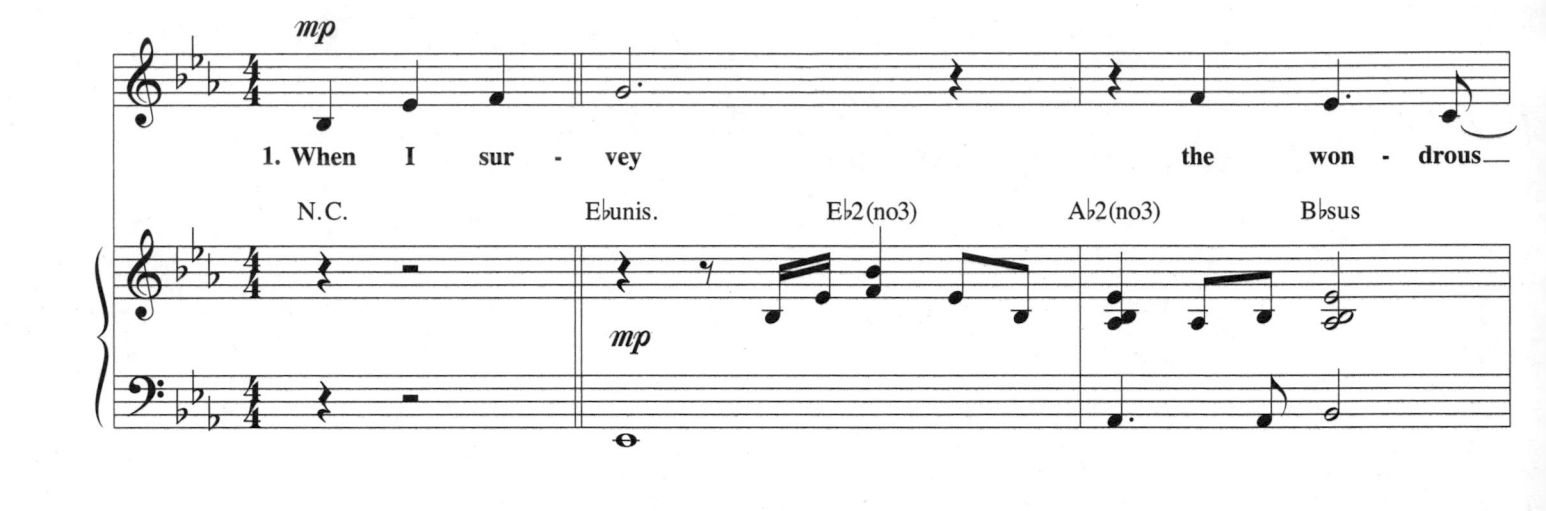

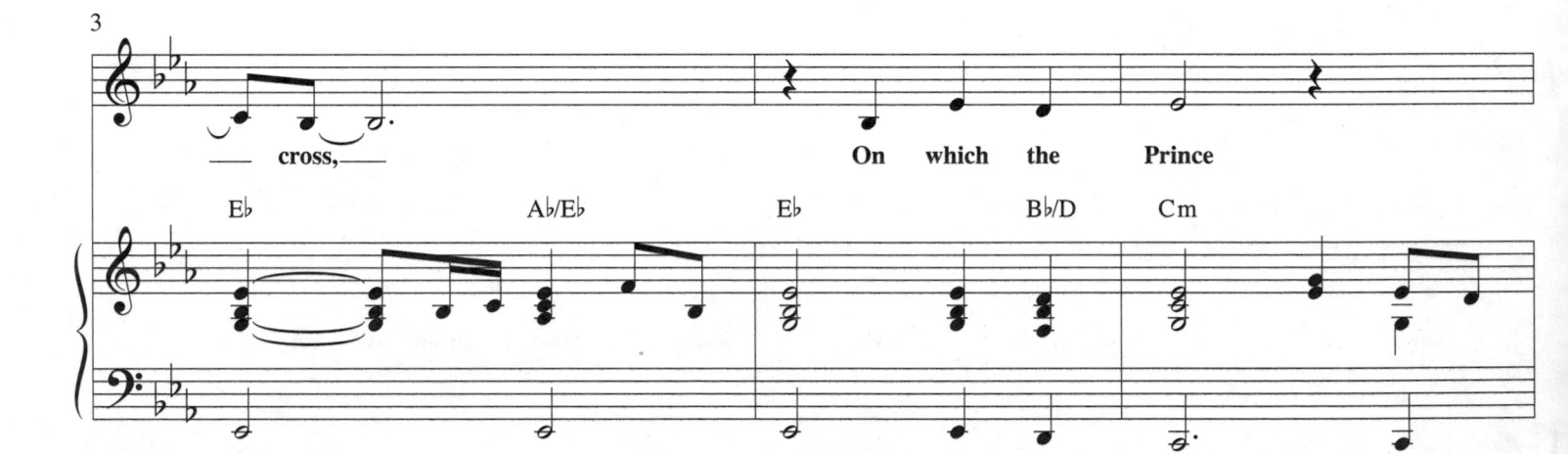